PENGUIN BOOKS

IN SEARCH OF A CHARACTER

Graham Greene was born in 1904 and educated at Berkhamsted School, where his father was the headmaster. On coming down from Balliol College, Oxford, where he published a book of verse, he worked for four years as a sub-editor on *The Times*. He established his reputation with his fourth novel, *Stamboul Train*, which he classed as an 'entertainment' in order to distinguish it from more serious work. In 1935 he made a journey across Liberia, described in *Journey Without Maps*, and on his return was appointed film critic of the *Spectator*. In 1926 he had been received into the Roman Catholic Church and was commissioned to visit Mexico in 1938 and report on religious persecution there. As a result he wrote *The Lawless Roads* and later, *The Power and the Glory*.

Brighton Rock was published in 1938 and in 1940 he became literary editor of the *Spectator*. The next year he undertook work for the Foreign Office and was sent out to Sierra Leone in 1941–3. One of his major postwar novels, *The Heart of the Matter*, is set in West Africa and is considered by many to be his finest book. This was followed by *The End of the Affair*, *The Quiet American*, a story set in Vietnam, *Our Man in Havana*, and *A Burnt-Out Case*. Many of his novels have been filmed, plus two of his short stories, and *The Third Man* was written as a film treatment. His most recent publications are *The Pleasure Dome* (1972), *The Honorary Consul* (1973), *An Impossible Woman: The Memories of Dottoressa Moor of Capri* (edited, 1975), *The Human Factor* (1978), *Doctor Fischer of Geneva or The Bomb Party* (1980), *Getting to Know the General* (1984) and *The Tenth Man* (1985). He has also written two volumes of autobiography, *A Sort of Life* (1971) and *Ways of Escape* (1980).

Graham Greene has written in all some thirty novels, 'entertainments', plays, children's books, travel books, and collections of essays and short stories. He was made a Companion of Honour in 1966.

GRAHAM GREENE

IN SEARCH OF A CHARACTER

TWO AFRICAN JOURNALS

PENGUIN BOOKS

in association with The Bodley Head

Penguin Books Ltd, Harmondsworth, Middlesex, England
Viking Penguin Inc., 40 West 23rd Street, New York, New York 10010, U.S.A.
Penguin Books Australia Ltd, Ringwood, Victoria, Australia
Penguin Books Canada Limited, 2801 John Street, Markham, Ontario, Canada L3R 1B4
Penguin Books (N.Z.) Ltd, 182–190 Wairau Road, Auckland 10, New Zealand

—

First published by The Bodley Head 1961
Convoy to West Africa' was published in *The Mint* in 1946
Published in Penguin Books 1968
Reprinted 1971, 1977, 1980, 1982, 1986

—

—

Set, printed and bound in Great Britain by
Cox & Wyman Ltd, Reading
Set in Monotype Times

CONTENTS

INTRODUCTION

I HAVE set two of my novels in Africa, *A Burnt-Out Case* in the Belgian Congo and *The Heart of the Matter* in Sierra Leone. The circumstances were rather different: I went to the Belgian Congo in January 1959 with a novel already beginning to form in my head by way of a situation – a stranger who turns up in a remote leper-colony. I am not as a rule a note-taker, except in the case of travel books, but on this occasion I was bound to take notes so as to establish an authentic medical background. Even making notes day by day in the form of a journal I made mistakes which had to be corrected at a later stage by my friend Dr Lechat. As a journal had been forced on me I took advantage of the opportunity to talk aloud to myself, to record scraps of imaginary dialogue and incidents, some of which found their way into my novel, some of which were discarded. Anyway for better or worse this was how the novel started, though it was four months after my return from the Congo before I set to work. Never had a novel proved more recalcitrant or more depressing. The reader had only to endure the company of the character called in the journal X and in the novel Querry for a few hours' reading, but the author had to live with him and in him for eighteen months. As one grows older the writing of a novel does not become more easy, and it seemed to me when I wrote the last words that I had reached an age when another full-length novel was probably beyond my powers.

The second journal, kept during the voyage of a convoy

to West Africa in 1941, was written for my own amusement at that period of the war when life and a future seemed uncertain for all of us. I had no book in mind, although during the voyage I remember reading a detective story of a fantastic kind by Michael Innes which set my mind moving in the direction of *The Ministry of Fear*, an entertainment which I wrote in what spare time from work I could allow myself in Freetown. It was my second visit to West Africa – the first had been in 1934 when I went up through Sierra Leone to the Liberian border and then walked across that strange country to the sea at Grand Bassa. My purpose now was work – government work of rather an ill-defined nature. During those months in Lagos and a year in Freetown I kept no journal for security reasons, and so I have no record of this bizarre period of my life, that included such episodes as a Police Commissioner driven out of his reason by well-meaning M.I.5 agents and my own quarrel with my superior officer two thousand miles away who ceased to send me any money to continue my work. God rest his soul! He is dead now and I was a sore trial to him.

I did not realize at the time that a novel would emerge from those years, and when five years later I began to write *The Heart of the Matter* I regretted my lack of notes. So many small details of life in Freetown had sunk for ever into the unconscious. I had stayed too long, so that I took too much for granted, for I have very little visual imagination and only a short memory. In *It's a Battlefield* the Assistant-Commissioner's journey from Piccadilly to Wormwood Scrubs had to be followed street by street, and with age the memory becomes worse. I had to make four visits of three months each to Indo-China for *The Quiet American*, but events prevented that in writing *A Burnt-Out Case*.

Neither of these journals was kept for publication, but they may have some interest as an indication of the kind of raw material a novelist accumulates. He goes through life discarding more than he retains, but the points he notes are what he considers of creative interest at the moment of occurrence.

ONE
CONGO JOURNAL

January 31st 1959

... All I know about the story I am planning is that a man 'turns up', and for that reason alone I find myself on a plane between Brussels and Leopoldville. The search for the character cannot end there – X must have known Leopoldville, come that way, but the place where he emerges into my consciousness is a leper station, many hundred miles up the Congo. Perhaps Yonda, perhaps one of the smaller stations four days away. I know no more about him yet than do his involuntary hosts. I cannot even picture the scene, or why should I be here? He is a man of means – perhaps he turns up by car, perhaps by a paddle-steamer, even perhaps by canoe. He flings himself with abandonment into the life of the leper-colony – is that a practical possibility? – but what his motives are I know no more than the priests and the doctors at the station. The novel is an unknown man and I have to find him: a situation that I cannot yet even vaguely imagine: a background as strange to me as it was to him at his first entrance.

February 1st, Sunday, Leopoldville

I am taken in charge at once by many strangers, but not the ones I had been warned to expect. A brand new city with miniature skyscrapers – I lunched fourteen floors up. Only outside the airport was there the smell of Africa – I smelt it first at Dakar on my way to Liberia in 1934 and always found it again, not only in the West, but on the airfield at Casablanca and the road beyond Nairobi. Heat? Soil? Vegetation? The smell of the African skin?

Lay down after lunch naked in the Sabena rest-house, but almost immediately I was woken by somebody knocking on the door. I put on a mackintosh and opened it on a young woman with so bad a stammer that for long I couldn't understand what she wanted. When she had gone the press arrived in relays.*

The streets of Leo outside the central area patrolled by tanks and lorries and black troops in single file reminiscent of the Indo-China war.

Dinner with a businessman. Inevitably he spoke of women and inevitably I encouraged him. The 'method' here seems to be to drive around the native town until a likely girl is seen and then to send the chauffeur with an offer of money. If she is married she will never come without her husband's consent. For birds in passage like myself a taxi-driver will always fetch a succession of girls, but it is necessary to be particular in description. There are a few 'free' women who receive men at home. Very low statistics of venereal disease. A black woman takes more care about the cleanness of her parts than a European. She is far more *pudique*, but on the other hand she is uncomplicated and in a relationship will never deny her man.

The same man who gave me dinner drove me around in the morning. In the native city (but one should talk here of

---

* There had been bad riots in Leopoldville two weeks before and nothing could persuade the journalists that my journey planned months ago was not occasioned by them.

cities, Leo one and Leo two, the old, the new) he told his chauffeur to take off his cap to be less conspicuous.* Up to the new university – Lovanium – a sense of great emptiness: will it ever be finished? Then round to the Stanley Memorial – a thick hideous statue where Stanley made his camp with a view of the Congo and the Pool. In the distance the skyscrapers and the new apartment houses.

'"And this also," said Marlow suddenly, "has been one of the dark places of the earth."'

Lunch with the Information Officer in his fourteenth-floor apartment. Talk of the Kibongoists who believe in the divinity of Kibongo, a man who died in prison in the forties in Elizabethville. Some attribute the present troubles to them. A B.B.C. type with wife and child in Brussels, fanatically keen, neurotically keen, on his job.

After the intrusion of the press, to the house of one of the rich young aristocrats of Leo. A beautiful young woman – long crossed thighs in her tight blue jeans, the wife of a middle-aged man in riding clothes, very rich, very self-made who makes crushers for the road, but with an intelligent eccentric face.

February 2nd, Coquilhatville

Met by Dr Lechat at the airport and brought to Yonda. A garden-city of 800 patients. At night the little groups round fires outside the houses. The doctor examining the dossiers, touching the skin, washing his hands in spirit, all here are

* This sounds a little sensitive to African feelings – it was not that. He was afraid that stones might be thrown.

contagious cases. If once the nerve ends are affected the fingers or toes are lost, though the disease can be checked there.*

Tired with the heat and too many strangers. The Bishop was at Yonda to celebrate the jubilee of a nun – I felt depressed.† My room seemed too bare with nowhere to hang clothes, and five large cockroaches in the communal shower. Why was I here? In the evening the Governor and his wife came for a drink – a motherly woman who wanted me to translate her books. She had written one and published it at her own expense. After dark the mosquitoes bad.

The story of the old Greek shopkeeper who saw his clerk in bed with his Congolese wife. He said nothing but went and spent his savings on an old car – so old that it would only start when pushed. Nobody could understand why he wanted it, but he said he wanted to drive a car once before he died, so they pushed him until the engine started and he went down to his square in Coq and hooted his horn to some of his clerks. He couldn't stop his car because then it would never have started again. He called to his clerk to wait for him, made the circuit of the square, twisted the wheel and drove over the clerk into his doorway. The clerk survived but with the legs crushed and the pelvis broken. The old man left the car where it was and waited for the police. It was the first case of the new young commissioner.

---

* As L. told me later many of those cases with mutilations were afflicted with a non-contagious type of leprosy, and even the degree of contagiousness of the so-called open cases is very controversial. The danger of leprosy has been much exaggerated.

† Hospitably, in the blazing heat of ten in the morning, the Bishop insisted on giving me whisky neat.

'What have you done?' he said. 'It is not a case of what I have done, but of what I am going to do,' the old man said, and shot himself through the head.*

February 3rd, Yonda

Everything suddenly changes. Woken in the dark to the sound of prayer and responses in the little chapel next door, then slept again till seven. Bright sunlight and the air still fresh. No cockroaches in the shower. The terribly tired priest – tall and washed-out with long elegant hands: teaches in a black seminary – only one other white man, apart from the teachers, in the whole region; the red-bearded priest, the stump of a cigar always in his mouth; the tough reserved lay brother who was in a Japanese prison camp – he gives the appearance of enmity, but in my story he begins to come alive as the one who speaks surprisingly at the very end in defence of X, my chief character.† As for the exhausted priest, what a life it must be to take one's rest in a leper-colony.

Arranged my room better with a coat-stand to serve as wardrobe. It begins to look like home. Walked down to the Congo. The great trees with their roots like the ribs of ships. From the plane they had stood out from the green jungle carpet browning at the top like cauliflowers. Their trunks curve a little this way and that giving the appearance of

* The economy of a novelist is a little like that of a careful housewife, who is unwilling to throw away anything that might perhaps serve its turn. Or perhaps the comparison is closer to the Chinese cook who leaves hardly any part of a duck unserved. This story – placed in Dr Colin's mouth – helped me to bridge a gap in *A Burnt-Out Case*.

† This idea was not followed.

reptilian life. Egrets like patches of arctic snow stand among the small coffee-coloured cattle. The huge Congo flowing with the massive speed of a rush hour out over the great New York bridges. This has not changed since Conrad's day. 'An empty stream, a great silence, an impenetrable forest.' From as far as one could see the little islands of grass flowed down towards the sea they would never reach – some as small as a bucket-top, some as large as a dining table. In the distance, coming out of Africa, they looked like families of ducks.* Two rusting metal boats. Blue waterlilies. A family sitting in a *pirogue* : the mother's bright yellow dress, the girl with a baby on her lap smiling like an open piano.

The Danish doctor who excavated in an old cemetery and found skeletons without fingers – it was an old leper cemetery of the fourteenth century. With the help of X-rays he made certain discoveries in the bone, especially in the nasal area, previously unknown. Now he is a specialist on leprosy and brings his skull to international conferences: it has passed many a *douane* in his baggage.†

At the end of my siesta came a rather rat-like man, a Fleming and a teacher in the Protestant school. He had written a novel in English and wanted advice about an agent. Is there any part of the world, in the most remote corner, where an author who is known will not encounter very soon one who wishes to be a writer? Do doctors en-

* Not grass as I learned later, but water-jacinth.
† Dr Møller-Christensen. He had been a legend to me when he was spoken of in Yonda, but later he was kind enough to send me his book, *Bone Changes in Leprosy*.

counter middle-aged men who still have the ambition of becoming doctors?

Dinner with the fathers: their tiny dartboard: the persiflage between the tired priest and the ex-prisoner who has relaxed a little. Water: soup: scrambled eggs: pineapple.

A motto of the local tribe: 'The mosquito has no pity for the thin man.'

February 4th, Yonda

A bad night. I could find no comfortable position on the hard mattress: a touch of rheumatism from the sweat: mosquitoes droning outside my meat-cover. Woke at six-forty to an overcast morning. Wrote to my mother and then took Julian Green's journal down to the Congo and found a place to read free from ants on board the rusty metal boat. Always astonished at the procession of grassy islands endlessly in progress at four miles an hour out of the heart of Africa, none, however small, overtaking another.

One priest in charge of constructions, one of education (the universal problem of what to do with the boy who has passed out of primary), the ex-prisoner, I think, of electricity. Is it possible that X (who is certainly no Olga Deterding as one imagines her to be) might be an architect? The drawings of the past he keeps concealed. Perhaps when he came he had illusions that he could work in the hospital. Go back to Europe, he is told, and have a six months' course in physiotherapy and massage – then we could make use of you. But he is afraid to return. They wonder –

19

but without worry – whether perhaps in his own country he is wanted by the police. He speaks French very badly and inevitably therefore his intimacy grows with the only priest who speaks English.*

Reading Julian Green one wonders whether it is easier for a homosexual to lead a chaste life, if he so wishes, because of the unfair stigma attached to his desire. Is it easier for him than for someone like X to refuse – from a religious motive – an affair which offers itself?

A Japanese atlas of leprosy: some of the plates resemble the warm landscapes of Van Gogh.

Through whose eyes shall I tell my story? It cannot be through X's, though I can imagine certain letters from women – condemnatory letters which perhaps in one of his rages he shows the priest. I don't think it can be through the priest's eyes – I wouldn't know this father and his daily routine well enough; I am suspicious of several points of view, except in so far as, like the letters and the dialogue, they are 'contained' in the story. There remains the author's 'I', but then he should not penetrate into the thoughts of any character – which must be indicated only in action and dialogue. This makes for the mood of mystery which I wish to catch. Title? possibly 'The Uncompleted Dossier'. If the priest keeps a dossier on X, it will enable us to penetrate a little into his mind. The one who must never put up a case for himself is X.

* I don't know why X, who later became Querry, lost half his English nationality.

Red beard never ceases to smoke except at meals: he stands around, bicycles around, strolls around, a veritable overseer. For the convalescent priest his breviary is a little like a cigarette, something to have between the fingers.

Visit to the dispensary of Dr Lechat.

The circle of leprosy – contagious and non-contagious are different diseases, but the non-contagious can develop into the contagious. If caught at the right moment of development the cure of the more serious cases is quicker than that of the non-contagious, but if that point is missed the position is very serious.

Reactions from treatment can be terribly painful and very serious – blindness, mutilation, etc., come from the accumulation of the drugs. Nodules are typical signs of contagious leprosy – on the ears, back, etc. The man without fingers (cured) who makes pullovers. Cortisone for reaction cases, DDS tablets daily through the mouth is the ordinary treatment* at a cost of a few shillings a year. The flirtatious girl who had had a surgical operation on her arms to cut the nerves† and who now suffers from a 'small palsy'. Her made-up fingernails.

Bacilli have to be cultivated – you cannot transmit to an animal. The social problem: the husbands are less inclined to follow their wives into a colony than the wives the husbands. The husband will set up in his village with another woman, and when his wife finds a lover to look after her in the colony, the husband descends demanding justice and the return of his *dot*. The Protestant missions

* Inaccurate. Corrected later.
† No. The sheath of the ulnar nerve.

21

allow this to happen, but the Catholic fathers give the husbands short shrift. People here are left alone and there are no moral inquisitions. Two husbands left cured and both wives are now being looked after by one man.

One of the little houses: a bedroom with two beds, very neat and clean under coverlets: the sitting-room with radio, bicycle, picture of King Baudouin, both Popes, a shop calendar (a girl advertising Singer sewing-machines), holy pictures.

It is strange how even the African is not acclimatized to this humidity and heat. Today is unusually bad, and so there is only a sprinkling of inert patients at the dispensary when otherwise there might be hundreds clamouring for attention.

Read a strange, terrible pamphlet 'The Social Stigma of Leprosy', by Doctor Eugene Kellersbergen.

Story of how a cultivated old gentleman in Paris – a friend of Gide – almost turned a doctor out of his apartment when he heard he was working on leprosy. 'You should have told me. I feel responsible to all the residents. How long will it be before I know whether I've caught leprosy?' He was seventy-four. 'Ten years.' 'Do you mean that I must live for ten years with this hanging over me?'

No bacilli have yet been found in non-contagious leprosy.(?)

The case of the leprophils – many volunteer workers but also many victims. The case of a European who contracted it very mildly, but because he boasted of it had to be transferred. He was told to keep his mouth shut this time, but again he told everyone and he had to be returned to Europe. The vanity of being something special – even in disease. Should one class Father Damien among the leprophils? The difficulty of catching leprosy shown by the 114 healthy people whom a German doctor (the forerunner of the doctors of Belsen) tried to infect at their own desire (they were to be expelled from Damien's island) with no success.

Vagaries of contagion: the two Texan soldiers of the same company who suddenly, after no contact with lepers, became infected. They had both been tattooed by the same man on Hawaii (?) and he had last used his needles on a leper.

The bacillus probably to be found in small quantities in healthy people who have spent a long period in certain parts of the world.

The lady who developed a mild leprosy. No question of her morality. But perhaps it had been enough in her case to handle a ball or some other object which had been handled by a leper.*
Memo to ask Doctor L. about the leprous prone.

In the evening the air was so humid that every now and then one felt it break on the skin like a single spot of rain. After dark storms broke around and there was rain but not

---

* The fathers had an idea that contagion might be carried by the breath and always in the confessional box held a handkerchief between their mouth and the leper's.

heavy rain. We were missed out. L. said that in six years he had known only about twenty days of such heat and humidity. Pursued by the schoolmaster who now tries to exercise a kind of spiritual blackmail.* I am replying that I am not competent in matters of faith: he should apply to a priest.

The atmosphere more relaxed when I had dinner with the fathers, perhaps because I am less shy and beginning to understand better the Belgian accent.

February 5th, Yonda

A very overcast day. The absence of the warning sun makes many people late for work.

As I shave a worker goes by in sandals cut to fit feet without toes: already I hardly notice that any more than I do the singing of the leper who is now painting the exterior of my door. The toeless man puts down his feet as though he were thumping the ground to level it with iron rods.

It is always depressing the first day in a very strange region knowing that weeks are to go by before one returns to the familiar, but after a few days (hold on and wait till they have passed) one has constructed the familiar in the very heart of the strange. One takes to routine as to

---

* I would claim not to be a writer of Catholic novels, but a writer who in four or five books took characters with Catholic ideas for his material. None the less for years – particularly after *The Heart of the Matter* – I found myself hunted by people who wanted help with spiritual problems that I was incapable of giving. Not a few of these were priests themselves. I can only attribute to the heat my irritation with this poor schoolmaster and to the fact perhaps that I was already beginning to live in the skin of Querry, a man who had turned at bay.

pleasure: after breakfast a shave, a letter to be written, perhaps an entry in the journal, then down to the Congo with a book to read on the old tin ship, return, another letter, a book, perhaps as yesterday a visit to the dispensary – it is almost time for lunch at the doctor's, then a siesta, a walk again to the Congo, the evening glass of whisky, dinner with the fathers, bed, another day rapidly gone. It is almost disturbing that today the routine will be altered, my meals reversed (lunch with the fathers), a visit to Coq for a *piqûre* and to make plans for my trip into the bush, drinks with the Governor.

The laughter of the African: where in Europe does one hear so much laughter as among these leper workers? But the reverse is true: the deep sense of despair one feels in them when they are sick or in pain. (I remember that too among my carriers in Liberia, my boys in Sierra Leone.) Life is a moment. This is their form of eternity.

Scene in the dispensary yesterday when there was too much noise of children crying and the doctor called to his assistant who commanded, 'Put the children to the breasts', a command, he says, you hear frequently at Mass. Certainly silence suddenly reigned.

Sufficiently overcast for walking. To the main dispensary and the new laboratory which is being built. L. showed me complicated apparatus for measuring to 1/20 thousandth of a second the reactions of the nerves. But what pleased him was a relatively cheap apparatus for taking the temperature of the skin simultaneously in twenty spots. A patch seems to have a higher temperature and he hopes that it will prove possible to forestall in a child the formation of a patch and begin treatment before a patch appears. In the same way he hopes to be able to foresee mutilation in the fingers and forestall it.

The man at the dispensary with elephantiasis: his feet and lower leg gnarled and noduled like an ancient tree trunk which has been carved at the end in the shape of huge toes.

If X has been a successful architect, isn't it possible that he has come to the end of his vocation? The love of his art has gone the way of his love of women: a kind of sensual exhaustion has overtaken that too.

After lunch went into Coq with the L. family and had my second T. and B. rather painfully at the National Health Service. Told of a man there who is continually ringing up the Sûreté at night to say that there are Congolese outside his house who have come to murder him and his wife. A lot of people at Coq now are sleeping with guns beside them – the chief danger is an incident provoked from fear.

Went to the Bishop's. A wonderfully handsome old man with an eighteenth-century manner – or perhaps the manner of an Edwardian boulevardier. He will try to lend me his boat for my trip into the bush.

Drinks at the Governor's: a simple kindly couple quite free from the vices of *colons*.* After dark an engine passes

* I learnt later that they had spent some twenty-five years in the Congo, almost always in the bush, in the early days without boat and without mail. They were on trek in the forest twenty days a month (that was the

26

through the streets spraying DDT s thickly that for a little we were lost in our cars completely as in any London smog: visibility down to a few yards. The Governor's *adjoint* with twenty years' experience. His admiration for the African woman. He spoke with emotion of the gentleness of life in the villages, but he feels – as I cannot – that the tribal framework must be broken and material incentives be given for that purpose. Doesn't this lead straight to the gadget world of the States? He spoke of the necessity for a mystique, but is there any mystique in America today, even inside the Catholic church?

February 6th, Yonda

Slept well for two hours, but then lay awake curiously uneasy – perhaps the effect of the *piqûre* – imagining that the distant voices among the leper houses meant danger. Lights flashed: I lost my torch and lay among illusions as thick and disagreeable as a DDT cloud. When at last I slept again I dreamt all the time of one person. How strange it is that for more than a hundred years Africa has been recommended as a cure for the sick heart.*

DDS given orally in tablets – two tablets three times a

---

duty), resting the ten other days in such small missions as I describe here. They taught the Congolese how to cultivate manioc and rice, supervising the building of dispensaries, inspecting native tribunals. Out of such experiences came the wife's book of stories which had to be published at her own expense, for we have seen how little interest there was in Belgium for her colonies. This is only one example of the tragic waste of small heroic lives.

* Even in the case of strong-minded Mary Kingsley. After the loss of her father and mother 'I went down to West Africa to die', she wrote.

week: an interval of one week at the end of a month. Hydrocarpus oil – of social use only in disguising the patches.

The constant conversation, ribaldry and laughter of the workers. If one could understand, the noise would become tedious, but incomprehensible it makes a kind of cacophonous background music.

A man whom L. has cured wrote a letter to his sister still in the leproserie urging the death of L. and boasting of what he had done in Leopoldville in the riots. The sister was frightened and couldn't understand and took it to a monitor at the school. Now another letter has arrived and L. wonders what is in it.

Another man whom he cured and who therefore had to leave the station threatened to burn down the doctor's house.

The wing of melancholia flicks at me today, perhaps because I have learnt nothing new here, perhaps because of my bad night, perhaps because of my dreams.

February 7th, Yonda

A good night with the help of a pill and only one dream. My *piqûre* nearly better and the wing of melancholy removed.

Pamphlet speaks of how Europe eradicated leprosy, but was it leprosy and was it eradicated?

Because of a delay in the cleaning of my shoes, I nearly missed the morning half-hour by the Congo. How easily a habit in strange surroundings takes on the character of a magic charm. Against what? Melancholy perhaps or ennui.

Reading the last volume of Julian Green's journal – *Le Bel Aujourd'hui* – with growing irritation. It seems to me impregnated with nothing so strong as spiritual pride but with spiritual vanity. He talks too much of God and the saints. In one passage he talks of a need to eliminate everything which is not pleasing to God. But is God pleased with a succession of pious platitudes on his nature? Wouldn't he give them all for one blasphemous line of Villon? I cannot help picturing the good God glancing at this book and throwing it aside as an author throws aside one more worthy and boring thesis on his work by a student for a baccalauréat.

Perhaps the first argument concerning X will be whether he should be classed as a leprophil. At the moment X stands still in my mind: he has hardly progressed at all. I only know a little bit more about his surroundings. Perhaps it will be necessary to name him – and yet I am unwilling to give him a definite nationality. Perhaps – for ostensible reasons of discretion – he should remain a letter. Unfortunately, as I learnt before, if one uses an initial for one's principal character, people begin to talk about Kafka.

Leprosy bacillus very similar to that of tuberculosis. Hansen's bacillus, however, cannot be transferred to an animal. Appearance: (*a*) patches with loss of sensation; (*b*) loss of sensation in the limbs without patches; (*c*) thickening of the skin of the face and ears, and the appearance of nodules. The last is a mark of the contagious.

Cleanliness is important to the non-patient: hardly at all to the patient.

When one travels far one travels also in time. A week ago at this hour I was still in Brussels, but I feel separated from that time by weeks not days. In 1957 I travelled more than 44,000 miles. Is it for that reason – I began my long journeys in the thirties – that life seems to have been quite interminably long?

Is there a way in which I can use the dreams of X? As I knew to my cost yesterday dreams can dictate the mood of a whole day and bring a dying emotion back to full life.

The Abokos. The Bishop told us two days ago that many were persuaded that with a certain powder they could destroy walls. They pushed the powder under their nails and then they had only to beat on a wall and it would fall. In primitive people as in children there is sometimes a failure to distinguish between dream and reality. This confusion is well illustrated in a huge novel *La Gana*, which I am reading now.

New drugs sometimes too expensive to be practical when dealing with millions. DDS costs only 3s. a year.

Colonial protocol. I have been told that at any gathering

– however casual and spontaneous, say in a restaurant – one cannot leave until one's seniors in rank have left. As was the case to my knowledge in Sierra Leone furniture is according to rank. L. will soon be in a position to have six instead of four armchairs or let his wife have a full-length mirror. The sad story of the man who couldn't have a second *cabinet* passionately wanted by his wife without passing certain exams and entering another grade. He failed and so out of his own money he built a second *cabinet* in the garden. But the garden belonged to the State and the Governor of the time told him to destroy it.*

The ceremony resuscitated of bringing an old-type coffin made in human form out of the forest. Only one man with memory of those days, the son of the old artifact. The whole thing a joke with the village: the coffin – of a man – very crude. The arms crooked at the elbows. The hair of head tied in two funeral knots. The colour of the face red. A small group of *colons*, including the burgomaster and his wife, taking photographs and sitting on tubular steel chairs from the sculptor's house. We had fetched an old priest, Father —, from his mission. The priest with the greatest knowledge of the *indigènes*. He made a small speech before this artificial ceremony which had for its purpose only the acquisition of one of these coffins for the

* In 1942 outside Freetown I lived in a house in a swamp used by the natives as a lavatory, a great encouragement to flies. (Once I closed my office window and killed 150 in two minutes.) I sent a demand for a native lavatory to the Colonial Secretary who replied that such a demand must come through the proper channels, but as in my case there were no proper channels I had to remind him of Mr Churchill's minute on the subject. I got my lavatory and was able to record on the Government files that like Keats my name was writ in water.

museum in Leo. Drums beat, old women danced with leaves, but one couldn't help comparing this scene, the tubular chairs and the whirr of an amateur cine-camera, with the real ceremonies and drums of Nicoboozu and Zigita in the untouched Liberian hinterland. There was only one genuine moment when the organizer and purchaser (for 2,000 francs) of the coffin wished to leave it in the village overnight and the people refused – it would bring bad luck. The notable of the district – with the air of a chief – a good-looking young Congolais in a smart European suit arrived hand-in-hand with his daughter, a beautiful girl in a yellow headscarf shaped round her head like a crown. She wore earrings, a European frock and a necklace, and she sat in her chair with the poise of a young queen while the wives of the *colons* chattered and moved restlessly here and there and fussed with their cameras.

The old priest stayed to dinner. A cheerful amusing old man, but as he was driven home afterwards in the dark he spoke of his fear for Coq, of what the unemployed and the *jeunesse* might start. We had a drink in the smaller of the two hotels after dropping him (the larger repelled by its yellow lights painted like the moon of a child's book with human features). Very discreet nineteen-twentyish pin-ups, a tiny dartboard. A man at the bar was impertinent to L. because he preferred to wait and signal the waiter rather than call 'boy! *Etes-vous muet?*' Returning saw the lit windows of the *fonctionnaire* who can't sleep at night for fear.

February 8th, Sunday, Yonda

Mass at six-thirty in the leproserie church: the Africans at the back. Segregation for health reasons? Taken in a bus driven by the beautiful nun whom I had seen in the *foyer social*. Melancholy on the horizon. How everything seems to be dying all the time in the tropics, if only a butterfly on the altar steps. What a mountain of *débris* there must be every day of mosquitoes, cockroaches, cockchafers, *moufes*, moths.

At breakfast spoke to the convalescent Father Henri. He would like to come with me on the Bishop's boat and get off at his seminary on the return voyage. Spoke of the Protestant and Catholic missions. The native is Protestant or Catholic according to the school in the neighbourhood, but he felt certain that there was a stronger credence in the Catholic, partly because of the cult of Our Lady, since the love of the mother is the chief element in the family. The mother is a constant, but the children may have many different fathers or be uncertain of the fathers. The seminary course too difficult for the Congolais: apart from French and Latin they are expected to learn Flemish too, with alternatives of German or English – in fact the whole European course of studies.

Drove with Doctor L. into the country. A family with a member in three branches of the public service who also make money by fishing and even by collecting caterpillars in the forest to sell at five francs a handful. The brothers do not live together, but they pool their money. Wives in town: girls in the country.

L. contradicts my acquaintance in Leo. Venereal

disease among women almost universal: only syphilis rare. Many cases now no longer react to penicillin.

At lunch L. called out to give serum to a man with snake bites. He's had several deaths from that cause.

In the evening to Coq to see some native dances arranged in a native bar for a *colon* who is leaving for Leo. Male dances called athletic, but these athletes would have been put to shame by any second class music-hall troupe in Europe. None the less they were watched by B., the district officer, with smiling proprietorial pride. How often have I seen that smile – like that of a proud schoolmaster watching a school performance of *The Merchant of Venice*, on the faces of British district officers or administrators, in West Africa, or Malaya . . . at least it is not the stupidity of the *colon*.

Returning I found my floor covered with big flying ants. A sign of rain? I remember them falling in showers over my food in Freetown just before the rain.

February 9th, Yonda

The rain came in the night.

I'm worried about my book. It's possible that for the *mise-en-scène* I should go back to my memories of Mosambolahun and Ganta in Liberia and my arrival at those places.

The arrival of X has to set the tone, and perhaps what L. would call a more 'sentimental' setting is required than this highly organized garden-city. I am worried too by the members of my priestly chorus: they are right for Europe but not for the missions. I have never yet found in a missionary priest either the naïvety which I want for certain of them, nor the harshness towards human failing, nor the inquisitiveness. These men are too busy to worry about motives – they are concerned with cement, education, electrical plant – not motives. How can I get rid of this falsity?

A morning with the doctor at the dispensary and hospital. The leaf-like tattooes on the faces of old women: the withered breasts like a pair of small empty gloves: the

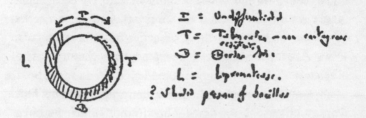

man without fingers or toes nursing a small child: the man with elephantiasis, testicles the size of a football: the tubercular woman (it seems unfair that if one is a leper one should suffer from other diseases as well): the old man with the sweet face and a gentle courtesy who has retired into the mud hut behind his hut to die (high blood pressure) – legs like a child and the face of a saint: the woman without legs who has borne a child: the man who retired to die and was not discovered at the back of his house for days.

Into Coq with L. to try to arrange about the boat. A terribly hot afternoon and a sense of despair. A funny little high-built boat badly needing paint like a miniature Mississippi paddle-steamer. Received by the retiring captain, a tall priest with gold-stopped teeth and a long straggling beard who gave us beer in the saloon with big windows above, I suppose, the bridge. A cupboard with a painted panel of the nativity.* There was a difficulty in sailing, it was explained; the boat had for long been in bad condition and now it was dangerous: a hole or a rotten plank (I'm not sure which) in the bottom. (Outside the cabin a life-belt looking like a dried eel all twisted out of shape.) Long discussion. A visit to Otraco† – all berths to Wafanya full as far as Ibonga. Possibility of car to Flandria and canoe to Ibonga where I could wait for the passenger-boat's return, or a plane to some other place, a car to Wafanya and return by passenger-boat, leaving out Ibonga. All tiring restless incomplete trips. Return to the cathedral. Only Monseigneur could give word for the boat to go, and the day before he had fallen and broken his hip. Conversation with the ambiguous Father André. Perhaps the boat could go next week – or next month. Apparently the captain, Father Pierre, is 'a captain who hates the sea'. On every trip (about four a year) something is wrong. Father A. agreed to speak to the Bishop. The answer: the boat is to be examined by two employees of Otraco and if they say it is safe it will sail. Otherwise no. I distrust the whole affair. I don't believe in a favourable decision.

Just as I sat down to dinner L. came in to say he had had a telephone call: all was well. I go on board Wednesday evening.

* This was used as an altar for daily Mass.
† The big trading company which maintained a service of cargo-boats with passengers on the Congo and its tributaries.

February 10th

Leprosy cases whose disease has been arrested and cured only after the loss of fingers or toes are known as burnt-out cases.* This is the parallel I have been seeking between my character X and the lepers. Psychologically and morally he has been burnt-out. Is it at that point that the cure is effected? Perhaps the novel should begin not at the leproserie but on the mission-boat.

How often people speak of the absurdity of believing that life should exist by God's will on one minute part of the immense universe. There is a parallel absurdity which we are asked to believe, that God chose a tiny colony of a Roman empire in which to be born. Strangely enough two absurdities seem easier to believe than one.

The cows with the elegant snow-white birds – *pique-boeufs*, not egrets – which attend them like guardian angels. The birds are so sleek and smooth that their feathers seem of porcelain. Innumerable butterflies.

The old woman with the palsied eyelids who could not blink. The doctor had bought her dark glasses but she would not wear them because they were not a medicine – she had trust only in drugs. The problem of shoes. Special shoes were brought for the mutilated but many people

* The English phrase is used by the Belgian doctors – there is no French equivalent, and for that reason I had to find quite a different title for my novel in French.

would not wear them. They wanted ordinary shoes. Even if they consented to wear shoes it was only on a Sunday, and usually they would accept them only to sell them.

The problem of charity. A special lepers' day in Coq produced enough clothes for four hundred patients, but there are eight hundred, so four hundred more had to be bought – a great expense. Then the four hundred given were all different, and this caused infinite jealousy.

The doctor is having six invalid chairs made for those who have lost their feet and can only crawl. But there are ten of these. How about jealousy, I asked him? 'For something important I will defy jealousy,' he said, 'but not for a tin of sardines.'

Names of Africans. Henry with a y, Attention, Deo Gratias.

Visit with L. to dispensary for an inspection of hands. He made the patients move their fingers in certain exercises. Treatment: paraffin wax, massage, splints. The typical monkey-hand due to a damaged medial* nerve. Surgical treatment, when the nerve is being strangled by a thickening of the sheath, to cut through the sheath and let the nerve free.

Haircut from Father Paul.

Men playing mysterious game altering the number of beans that lie in rough troughs on a home-made board.

* No. Ulnar nerve.

A coil of caterpillars brought home by a leper to sell or eat.*

Palsy and mutilation alternatives. A man goes on working with dead nerves and injures his fingers because they feel nothing: palsy where the nerves react is some sort of protection.

February 11th, Yonda

Everyone quiet and depressed.

The leper tribunal outside a house – three men, representatives of their tribes, listening to the witnesses. They can hear small cases of theft, abuse, stealing a man's wife, and they can sentence to short terms in the prison near Yonda. But the prisoners are allowed out for work and treatment: they only spend the nights in the prison.

Shopping for the boat – DDT bombs, eau-de-cologne, soap-flakes, ten whiskies, thirty-six soda.† Gave the L.'s dinner in the hotel. The terrible bar with steel chairs and man-in-the-moon lamp-shades. The dinner not so bad.‡

* The coil of pale caterpillars reminded me of the long nails of an old Chinese in the post office at Kuala Lumpur. He carried his left hand under his armpit: the five nails, each a foot long, grey-yellow and semi-translucent, were so intercoiled that they gave the effect of wriggling movement.

† It had always been my experience in Europe to find whisky the favourite drink of the clergy, but on board the captain only drank beer, Father Henri would not take more than one glass before dinner, and the rest was left to me. The soda water was at any rate useful for cleaning teeth, for the Congo water was the colour of clay.

‡ One of the saving graces of the Congo was the excellent cheap wine obtainable, even in Coq. I remember in particular an excellent Portuguese *rosé*. Whisky only cost the equivalent of about twenty-two shillings. Camemberts flown from Europe were creamy and mature.

Then whisky on the boat. The Bishop's cabin very pleasant. The altar in the deck-house.

The Bishop's accident. In all the years before he had never known illness, and the boredom rather than the pain is killing him. He had been a man who could not stand being alone: as a bishop dignified and immaculate with a big cross round his neck. A kind and courteous man who had very little faith in his diocese. Now he lies in his pyjamas with his intolerable ennui, unable to understand how to be alone. In all the fifty years since his ordination solitude has never caught up with him before. He is unable even to move his head without pain.*

At the last moment a local mail brings a letter from another local writer with a copy of his book published at his own expense. Why should this dream of writing haunt so many? The desire for money? I doubt it. The desire for a vocation when they find themselves in a life they haven't really chosen? The same despairing instinct that drives some people to desire rather than to experience a religious faith?

February 12th, on the Bishop's boat

Reading a book which moves me, *La Fête Espagnole*, by Rey.† Woken at five by the boat leaving and opened my

---

* I am glad to say that the Bishop recovered from his broken hip. The apparent *boulevardier* of smooth colonial days came into his own in troubled times. He has stayed at his post, has the confidence of the Congolais and has remained firm through all the troubles, helping the white people who have remained in Equatoria. How often the lives of individual priests reproduce in this way the history of the Church.

† The author is said to have been depicted as the principal character in the French best-selling novel *Le Repos du Guerrier*.

window to see the lights of Coq. A lot of vibration from the paddle. The river about one and a half kilometres wide. We keep near one bank.

A control at the entrance of the Ruki river to see that the ship is clear of flowers and plants which might seed and help to close the channel.

A pontoon on either side loaded with logs. The former captain reads his breviary after breakfast. X's account of his deliberate affair with a young married woman in order to ease his own pain. At the end he tries to go back to sexual love, but rejects it from sheer lack of desire. One leaves him waiting for what may come.*

There are three priests on board, and the African hands, who seem to include at least one woman. There is Père Henri, the convalescent, a former captain himself, who has come for the trip but is longing to reach by daylight his seminary at Bakuma; the retired captain, Père Fierre, with his long ragged beard and glasses, who is joining the seminary as a professor, and Père Georges, the new captain – a man obsessed with shooting. There is a kind of monkey near here which lives on the ground and he boasted of how many he had shot on one round-up – apparently they are very good to eat. Just now we passed a cormorant – long neck and tiny head – sitting on a log and he took a shot at it, but the vibration of the boat made him miss and it flew off the way we had come, keeping always the same distance above the water. Apparently the crocodiles here are long-nosed and not man-eating. Bathing is safe. This according to the fathers: the doctor doubted their dependability.

* These ideas were abandoned or completely transformed.

The first day one watches to see whether a routine will emerge: it is a routine that makes home. You can have moments of excitement, ecstasy, happiness, but you can't have the sense of peace.

At eleven we had beer and then I taught the fathers 421. After lunch siesta.

Reading Conrad – the volume called *Youth* for the sake of *The Heart of Darkness* – the first time since I abandoned him about 1932 because his influence on me was too great and too disastrous. The heavy hypnotic style falls around me again, and I am aware of the poverty of my own. Perhaps now I have lived long enough with my poverty to be safe from corruption. One day I will again read *Victory*. And *The Nigger*.

The colour of the water a polished pewter: the clouds seem to shine upwards from below the pewter surface. Even the green of the woods lies under the pewter. Some fishermen's houses on stilts remind one of the East.* Men standing in *pirogues* have their legs extended by their shadows into the water, so that they have the appearance of wading. Has some rationalist suggested this as an explanation of Christ walking upon the water?

* I was thinking, I suppose, of a particular village on the Mekong river in Laos, not far from Luang Prabang, where the motor of my canoe broke down. It was during the Indo-China war and we were trying to reach a particularly holy Buddhist shrine, there to offer our prayers against the advancing Viet Minh army. I remember with vivid pleasure the meal on the floor of one house on stilts, and how the walls were covered with *Paris Match* photographs of Queen Elizabeth's coronation, though our peasant host could not speak a word of French. I do not apologize for such digressions. Memories are a form of simile: when we say something is 'like' we are remembering.

More and more worried the last few days whether anything will come of this book. Perhaps I am not accepting the reality but struggling against it, and at the same time I am frightened of what the doctor calls 'sentimental', which is his word for picturesque or dramatic. Perhaps X helps with hand-exercises and is caught forgetting the obvious precautions of washing with spirits. The priests are more concerned with engineering, electricity, navigation and the like, than with the life of man or God – but that is X's wrong impression. He has come seeking another form of love and is faced with electric turbines and problems of building, and he fails to understand the priests as much as they fail to understand him.

The water at the bow of the pontoons the colour of burnt-sugar.

A first sentence perhaps: 'Each day after breakfast the captain read his breviary in the deck-house.'*

The continuous shovelling of wood from pontoon to engine reminds one of the Atlantic crossing by Phineas Fogg.

The approach to Bakuma and the excitement of Père Henri: 'my home'.
'Not your prison?'
'No. Yonda is my prison.'

* The book was coming nearer. Indeed the second sentence was very like to this: 'The captain in a white soutane stood by the open window of the saloon reading his breviary.'

Arrival. Dinner in the mission and afterwards the fathers played a card game, with three packs, which they called Matches. You could deal five – ten – fifteen – twenty cards, and the stakes were made with matches. The total stakes must not equal the number of cards in the hand, and one must make exactly the number of tricks staked, neither more nor less. As there are three aces in each pack, etc., they have orders of value according to the colours of the pack, red, white and blue.

A disturbed hot night in spite of the pill. Dreamt angrily of someone of whom I have never waking thought angrily.

Conrad's *Heart of Darkness* still a fine story, but its faults show now. The language too inflated for the situation. Kurtz never comes really alive. It is as if Conrad had taken an episode in his own life and tried to lend it, for the sake of 'literature', a greater significance than it will hold. And how often he compares something concrete to something abstract. Is this a trick that I have caught?

It was curious tonight to think what professions one would have attributed to these fathers if one had not known – only one man in a soutane. Father Georges, the captain, resembles very closely many young officers of the Legion one has known in Indo-China; Father Pierre rather resembles W. G. Grace or perhaps Huxley; the others I would have divided between young doctors and dons (in the last category would have come the Austrian who was a prisoner of the Americans after the war – he cannot talk quite comfortably of Germany. Incidentally Martin

Bormann's son is somewhere here in the bush). A kind of euphoria among the fathers. Continual jokes and laughter. Only one young man (one of the few beardless), a little quiet and self-contained. Does this continual badinage and college humour go on through all the years?

A mission is a little like a consulate. There is always a portrait of the new Pope and a portrait of the bishop.

Can I make a value out of this euphoria, the continual jests and laughter around the enigmatic and unresponsive figure of X?

February 13th, Bakuma

Woken by the sanctus bell from the deck-house. Breakfast at the mission and then a walk with Father Pierre. People who ran up to him to shake his hands: they could not understand why I did not speak their language – he had to explain. Others who knelt and crossed themselves. A girl with beautiful heavy breasts made me aware of how sex was returning after satiety, slowed by the heat and the strangeness but returning. Another girl with nipples like billiard balls. The strange realization that at Yonda one had never shaken hands: I had got used to the sick and the contagious.

The almost deserted fishing village where a man and a woman were squeezing the juice out of sugar cane: the sap enclosed in a leaf and then twisted by a piece of wood into a trough. Bees swarming round the fibrous sap, but apparently they seldom sting. The father lifts his soutane and takes a leap over a colony of red ants on the march. Hibiscus flowers.

From the boat planks are being unloaded and wood taken on board, the seminarists helping.

I don't know why but a recurring dream of mine comes back to mind, that my mouth is full of vegetation, which I drag out in great handfuls and there is always more to come.

Longing to get away from this mission station, but now at eleven-thirty they have only finished unloading the planks and begun on the fuel. This probably means lunch at the mission: another meal of raillery in incomprehensible Flemish and hardly more comprehensible French.

Melancholy shows signs of returning, perhaps because of my dream.

The woman on the pontoon washing and pounding her cotton sarong, the sarong she wears catching between her buttocks: a memory of Fotis stirring the pot in *The Golden Ass*.

The lovely smile of black women and the flirtation of their eyes.

At 2.10 p.m. at last away. Terribly hot. Uneasy siesta.

After an hour and a bit stopped at a village Ikonga to buy cooking pots. A lovely young woman in green with a fish.* Photographs. Gathering storm. Father Henri bathes. Thunder and lightning and heavy rain and the steam blew a joint as we prepared to leave. Held up for the night. The

* I asked Father Georges whether perhaps I could buy her as a wife for the trip, but he explained that it would be hardly worthwhile. Any child would belong to the mother and for the birth she would return to her family. If I still wanted her then, I would have to put down the marriage price all over again.

46

captain stretched in a deck-chair and read his breviary. Father Henri walked up into the village to tell the people that there would be Mass in the morning. The captain went fishing. A lovely fresh evening.

When the lamps were lit some old women came creeping in to confession.

The accident to the pipes has happened on Friday February 13th. Has there been a Friday February 13th since 1942 when I fell down an open drain in Lagos?

February 14th, on the River Ruki

In the early morning (6.10), as we start after two Masses, the river smokes with mist near the bank. Up before light when the siren blew at five to signal the first Mass. A lamp-lit procession came down from the village. The captain said the first Mass. Men working in the engine-room came in for the Elevation and went back to work again. Eggs and bacon for breakfast, and the captain skinned one of the rabbits Father Henri brought on board yesterday in a hutch.*

The book moves a little. Opening: the doctor and the burnt-out cases: a bitter discontented man, tired of the raillery of the priests, unable to do what he wants to do: a hard smoker of cheap cheroots. This is the opening. Question, to turn to the boat and X in passage down the river or to carry straight on to his arrival? I incline to the first.†

* The seminary had quite a rabbit farm. Father Henri, who had a touch of cruelty, had named one rabbit Brigitte Bardot.

† In fact I abandoned the idea of beginning with the doctor, who seems in the writing to have lost his discontent and his cheroots.

Is the doctor perhaps married? To a foreigner – the same nation as X. As X's past comes out the doctor becomes obsessed by jealousy. It is he, not one of the priests, who worms the past out of X and misunderstands. If it is to be a choice between X and the doctor, of course the mission have to choose the doctor. Who is a good man. Spoilt by frustration, that's all. So the man who is seeking a new form of love finds a new form of hate.*

The African hair which looks as though it will never grow enough to demand any effort in fact needs constant attention. A barber is always at work on the pontoon with comb and safety-razor blade, scraping, while his client holds a mirror constantly before him to see the work as it is done.

The boat all the way escorted by butterflies.

Reading *The Roots of Heaven*, an admirable book if only it were not quite so obviously modelled on the language and method of Conrad. A French Marlow.

One searches the forest for a sign of life, other than butterflies, rather as one searched when a child those puzzle-drawings in which a human face was concealed.

Ingende at lunch time. Walked up with Father Henri and posted letters. By the beach a notice in French, Flemish and *indigène*: 'Zone of sleeping sickness. Be careful of the tsetse fly.'

* Another abandoned intention.

The photograph above the Bishop's bed in which I sleep of a church or cathedral covered in snow.

At the end of *The Burnt-Out* * we have a jealous husband (without reason for jealousy) who drives X away from his attempt at rehabilitation. But the doctor's wife pursues him to Coq, Leo, Brazzaville, perhaps with the sentimental idea of 'atoning'. She understands as little as her husband. She offers herself and of course he doesn't want what she offers – which to the husband is the worst insult of all. He kills him and she becomes the heroine of a crime of passion in a classic African scene. What cannot be read at the trial, for it would destroy the picture, is X's last letter – to one of the priests at the leproserie, or perhaps to his mother who had never burnt-out, or to both. Am I going too far from the original vague idea: am I beginning to plot, to succumb to that abiding temptation to tell a good story? Yet I feel that X must die because an element of insoluble mystery in his character has to remain. Of course he could simply walk off like an early Chaplin.†

Arrived at Flandria around three. Two fathers came on board and drove me to L.'s, the manager of the United Africa factory. Ex-Indian army officer still young. Intelligent and very pretty wife. Two children at Coq and two small ones who greeted us – it was unfortunately the hour

---

*I had nearly found the title I wanted.

† As the novel came patchily into consciousness the doctor refused to act this jealous role. He soon lost his wife as well as his cheroots, which returned to their rightful owner, the father superior. Eventually a *colon* took his place as the jealous husband.

of the Saturday siesta. The small boy had celebrated his birthday the day before and he told at once of his presents – a hammer, saw, nails, and showed with pride what he had made: a doll's bed, a stool, a bird-house. The small girl stood on her head and was sick. Drank a great deal of beer. A travelling salesman for a beer company turned up unexpectedly. We made a rendezvous with the boat and then drove round the estate. The mill – nothing wasted: all that is not crushed into oil is fuel for the furnaces: no other fuel required. A smell of stale margarine.* Huge areas of forest clearance like a scene on the Western front. Platforms have to be built some eight feet up the trees to cut them off above the great ribs. A cook who had leprosy in the feet and had to be dismissed because of the children and who wept.

The boat punctual at the rendezvous looked very beautiful coming round the bend of the river into the sunset-stained reach.

A very hot night in the deck-house because we had to have the veranda doors closed for steering in the dark, so I went to bed early and had bad dreams.

A lot of singing in the dark: Africans sing the events and characters of the journey. It is a possible opening to begin with a native song, 'Here is a man who is not a father nor a doctor. He comes from a long way away and he goes to blank. He drinks much and he smokes and he gives no man a cigarette.'†

* There was nothing in common between my intelligent and charming host and the unspeakable Rycker, but at Rycker's factory too 'through the net of the window there blew in the smell of stale margarine'.

† Another abandoned beginning. The beginning of a book holds more apprehensions for the novelist than the ending. After living with a book

February 15th, Sunday on the Momboyo River

We travelled all night and I only woke at six to find the first Mass nearing an end.

I can never get used to the beautiful even colour of the young African women – the most beautiful *backs* of any race. Here there are elaborate crossroads of partings on the scalp, the hair is twisted in thin cords to form a kind of bird's cage. The big toes often made up.

What Lechat told me our last evening about suicide among leprologists – a common phenomenon. The doctor who soaked his house and himself in petrol and then set himself on fire. The doctor who injected himself with an enormous dose of snake venom.

The bitter doctor of my story – Doctor Colin – breaks out on this subject – 'And perhaps you are waiting for me to kill myself.'*

The sisters who sometimes resent leprosy being cured. ' It's a terrible thing – there are no lepers left here.'

---

for a year or two, he has come to terms with his unconsciousness – the end will be imposed. But if a book is started in the wrong way, it may never be finished. I can remember at least three novels I have abandoned, and one abandonment at least was caused by a wrong opening. So one hesitates a long time before taking the plunge – whether one is to sink or swim depends on that moment.

* No such bitterness was ever shown in the book by Dr Colin – the case of a character who would not conform to the plan.

Stopped for a quarter of an hour at a village. The *maison de passage* with its medley of objects: a crucifix, a Catholic prayer book and magazine, a Protestant mission paper, a coloured pin-up of Jane Russell which turned out to be the backing of a looking-glass made in Hong Kong.

The healthy-mindedness of the young has now robbed men of their periodic rest: where we used to have four or five days in a month, we cannot now expect more than two.

I missed this morning's crocodile – of course the first instinct of Father Georges was to shoot at it as he shot at the cormorant, and I couldn't detect the fishing eagle he pointed out on a tree stump.

Now it's a heron and alas! this time the captain's aim is true. It flaps and tries to rise and sinks into the water. The boat is put about. I can't help remembering the late Cardinal Griffin at a dinner at Dick Stokes's opposing a Blood Sports Bill which was under discussion on the ground that animals were created for man's pleasure as well as for his use.*

Remember: the dog at Mass. The captain sitting in the veranda doorway, the dog behind him, chatting to the black crew below.

With the dark we came to Imbonga and another Father Henri, with untidy red hair and bloodshot eyes and little red beard. I liked him. Sitting drinking in the deck-house by lamplight one touched the right mood. Went on shore

---

* And if that is a correct view in moral theology, to Hell I would say to moral theology.

to eat and sleep, but slept very badly. Also visited the sisters, and the priests insisted on arranging a car to take me to the leproserie seven kilometres away, but I had my own intentions.

Ate Father Georges's heron for dinner, but I mistook it for a rabbit.

February 16th, Imbonga

After breakfast walked to the leproserie; a guide led me to a fork through two kilometres of forest and showed me the path to take. After he left a big monkey, red with a long tail, leapt across the path ahead. To the leproserie in one hour five minutes, which was brisk walking. Three villages. Saw round them all with the black *infirmier* and his two assistants. No doctor. One nun who bicycles daily through the forest from Imbonga. The main village very well laid out with room for three lines of traffic – if there had been any traffic – with a wide arena of palm-trees down the middle. The lepers brushing the dust from the empty street. There remain even today nightmare cases. Went into one hut divided into two rooms: the inner room completely dark – one could just distinguish a pot and hear the sounds of human movement. Then there emerged an old woman on hands and knees (if you could call them hands), like a dog, unable to raise her head, just crawled towards the sound of human voices. The only word I knew was *ouane – bonjour* – a stupid phrase in that context. A cheerful old man at the beginning of the village waved his stumps and lifted mutilated feet. I was dashed a dozen eggs for which I paid and had a cheerful leper to carry them and walk back with me – bad lesions on the forehead and one eye nearly closed. Unmarried. He had been six years in the leproserie.

Siesta interrupted by arrival of car and so unwillingly, because it was siesta time and I had seen all I wished, back to the leproserie (my camera stuck and I had to leave it behind). It was amazing that a car could get there along the last part of the route – the narrow paths and the narrow bridges, but it did.*

Later after seeing round the mission a storm broke and out of the rain emerged a regional officer and a young doctor (with a copy of *The Third Man*), who had arrived by what they call here a *canot* as distinct from a *pirogue* – we would call it a motor boat. So people seem to merge in Africa – out of the vastness for a night, whisky and 421. Back to the boat to sleep, but slept badly. A belief that I had mice in my mattress.

Father Henri talking of African materialism had a good school story. The master was showing his class a globe and telling them about the earth and the countries on it. Then he asked for intelligent questions. Boy at once put up his hand. 'How much did the globe cost?' 'I want *intelligent* questions.' Another boy put up his hand. 'What's inside it?'

Father Henri's whimsical passion for tormenting the cat of the mission and the dog in small ways.

* I had the forest outside Imbonga in mind when I described Querry's search for Deo Gratias, mingled perhaps with memories of the deeper forests of Liberia.

February 17th, on the River

Off again and glad to be back on the boat. The whole river, much narrower now, steams a foot from the surface. Along one edge the white nenuphars stand like birds. A few small crocodiles lying along the fallen branches and diving as the boat passes.

The L.'s had lent me *The Tiger in the Smoke* – a most absurd unreal story by Margery Allingham. It didn't even pass the time: it was an irritation.

An ibus to add to my natural history list.

Lusaka. We take on wood. A madman in a red fez and a yellow-green robe wearing a crucifix, a dagger and a big plaque and carrying papers with a great air of importance. Obviously nothing can go on without his presence. Like ourselves he believes himself to be in control. Once he knelt and crossed himself. (Like ourselves too he is in control under God.) The pretty young girl who goes ashore and stands alone rubbing her back and buttocks against a tree stump.

The madman gets cross with the labourers and comes on to the pontoon: he hands his papers to the captain – a guide for the use of *infirmiers*, plans of the blood stream and the digestive system. When I tried to photograph him he posed at the tiller.

Remember: the innumerable questions on the road Africans exchange and then go opposite ways asking and replying without even turning round, their voices carry so clearly.

The madman gives his last instructions as we prepare to put off, then retires to a hut on the bank, and someone obediently surrenders the one deck-chair. He seats himself, crosses himself; thanks to him everything is in order. There is something parliamentary about him. Then he stands on the point of the shore waving us on. He wears sun glasses, but there is only one lens left, and as well as his medical handbook and an official envelope, he has a tin box - holding what?

Reading *The Cruise of the Nona*. I cannot like Belloc. He exaggerates everything. He talks a lot about Truth, but there is no truth in his feelings. When he exaggerates his hatred he achieves a rather crude comic effect, but when he exaggerates his feeling for what he loves, we are aware of a fundamental falsity. Certainly he wants to believe, but does he?

In the evening heard over the radio news of the disturbances in Brazzaville: one feels that European Africa is rapidly disintegrating. To hear such news three hundred miles within the bush surrounded by Africans is a little like one of the science-fiction stories of Ray Bradbury.

Went to bed early. We pulled out about ten for the night at Wakao.

February 18th, on the River

A good night thanks to the supponeryl which I had left in

the fridge. Stopped at breakfast time and a *colon* came on board – a little man in glasses who is married (really married) to an *indigène* who only speaks her own tongue. Four children and of course all the relatives, but it matters little – he has made his choice of living his whole life in Africa.

At 9.15 we stop again by a beach. The captain rides off into the bush on a bicycle to find if possible a cargo from a *colon*, for the boat is empty.

Belloc's attack on Parliament: if one shared Belloc's temperament of suspicion one would speculate whether he had been bribed to attack Parliament for the *wrong* reasons so that people might forget the real issue – which is not, after all, the corruption of individual ministers or members.

Now started re-reading *David Copperfield*. Surely the first two chapters are supreme in the novel: untouched even by Proust or Tolstoy. One dreads the moment when Dickens will fail as he always fails – with exaggeration, whimsicality, sentimentality. How perfectly the idyll of Yarmouth is put in, with the menace of Mr Murdstone in the background.

This afternoon has been too hot, with the river narrowing to fifty yards or less. Now at five Father Georges, the captain, sits stringing a rosary, Father Henri plays patience. The book stays stationary in my mind.

A *colon* couple with their child came on board soon after dinner.

February 19th, on the River

A lot of tsetse flies with their nasty little jet-styled wings.
Père Georges has just shot – it took two balls – a beautiful
fishing eagle. He always shoots a sitting target, and never
one on the wing. The bird was only wounded. The boat
stops. An African swims ashore and finishes the bird off –
from a very discreet distance – with a log of wood. Then he
swims back with it and immediately they begin to pluck it.
Too tough for our eating.

Reading a difficult (for me) odd book *La Forêt Veuve* by
Silvagni about Brazil. Fine description of a kind of country
brothel – two women and musicians to each house and an
elaborate ceremonial. '*Il faudrait être le dernier des cons et
des salauds pour les appeler putains, les Dames Amies.
Ou alors, putain, c'est le plus beau compliment qui peut
être fait à une femme, à une vraie femme, par un vrai
mâle.*'

Little birds blue-black in colour like swallows.

Into the eighth day and I really feel I've had enough. I'd
like to be transported to a bathroom in the Ritz in Paris and
then to a dry Martini in the bar.

Arrived about four at Wafanya. One priest, the Superior
there, the others away. A big untidy mission and a big
untidy man with a cigar. Very, very hot. Thirty degrees
even at sunset.* Decided to sleep on the boat.

* 86° Fahrenheit.

The three *Assistance Sociale* women, and Father Octave, from the leproserie came for drinks in a Volkswagen and I said I would spend the week-end with him. A very sympathetic man of a peasant farmer stock.

February 20th, Lombo Lumba

Lombo Lumba means a clearing in the forest and the leproserie is only that, picturesquely studded with rounded red hills covered with foliage which are the work of the termites. Drove out early with the fathers of the boat and walked all round till well after ten. Terribly hot. Great sense of width and airiness in spite of the heat. A children's home where the children are segregated from birth – the mothers come twice a day to feed them and have little desks to hold their cleaning material. Neither the women nor the small children in this region attractive. The poor little wasting creature, four years old, without speech, crouched in a womb position on a bed in an empty dormitory, as small or smaller than a year-old child, and a permanent unresponding misery on his face. Fathers allowed to visit on Sundays.

The fathers from the boat departed. The obvious loneliness of Father Octave made him very sympathetic. Reads cheap *romans policiers. Cafard* particularly in the evenings. After my siesta we walked again, but it was almost unbearably hot, into the forest, to his favourite pond. He had built a small bench there to sit on with his *cafard*. Then the fathers from the boat turned up again (Father Henri ill from the sun) and there was 421. At 7.15 rosary in a little out-of-door grotto by the light of candles. Memo: in the church the lepers' benches are made of cement to make them easier to wash down.

Supper with the *demoiselles*, as the women of the *Assistance Sociale* are called.* Then for my benefit the school band came with torches and the larger boys put on a kind of show. Much more psychological help given here than at Yonda. Flower gardens planted too. Everything to raise the spirits.† All day as we walked around questions shouted as to who I might be. The father replied, a big fetishist. Played 421 with the father and the *demoiselles* till after ten. A huge spider in my room and woken by a real tropical storm which did not stop till six.

To my delight, for I am tired of all this, it was agreed that the boat should start back after lunch at Wafanya.

February 21st, Lombo Lumba

Encouraged by the thought of going. Walked around taking photographs for the sake of appearances, talked with increasing difficulty (how it adds to the fatigue of a tropical journey to struggle with a foreign tongue). Played 421 and lost every game. It almost makes one superstitious to watch how the priests win always.‡ At last it was 11.30,

---

* This as far as I could make out is a kind of lay order, with vows of chastity, but no permanent vows.

† The voice of my sceptical doctor might add, 'If Africans' spirits can be raised by flowers'. At any rate any psychological aid given to the white man or woman in these dismal circumstances is of value.

‡ After the preliminary game to show them the rules, I lost every game on the boat to Father Georges and Father Henri, and yet we must have

time to go to Wafanya, the whole company – *demoiselles* and all. At last – 12.45 – off with a lot of deck passengers, goats, etc. Half an hour later we stupidly struck a snag in mid-stream and bent the rudder. Now we are tied up to the bank in the forest, the rudder must be unshipped, a fire lit, and *perhaps* it will be possible to straighten it. Frustration and heat! The long fingers of the palm leaves quite still which in the smallest suspicion of a breeze begin to play like fingers on a piano.

For book:

'The passenger wrote in his diary: "I am alive because I feel discomfort." He was uncertain why he kept the diary. Perhaps – "I feel fear, but it is of small things: the cockroach in my cabin . . .".'*

Sat for relief from the heat on the pontoon in the dark while the captain fished. The stars became visible one by one and the large vampire bats went creaking over the forest. Difficult to sleep at first because of all the livestock.

February 22nd, Sunday on the River

Got off at last about 6.15. Woke with a very sore throat. Mass. A tall rather insolent-looking African had a prayer

---

played at least four games a day. I was introduced to the game in Saigon or Hanoi by officers of the Sûreté who had the job of shadowing me and who therefore perhaps allowed me a proportion of victories.

* The dreaded essential opening sentences have almost arrived. The actual one: 'The cabin-passenger wrote in his diary a parody of Descartes: "I feel discomfort, therefore I am alive", then sat pen in hand with no more to record.'

book with small holy pictures, including a film star dressed as a cowboy.

Today at nine it is dark and cool and stormy, but to make up there are quantities of tsetse flies. Almost too dark to write.

The storm broke heavily and has been going on for an hour and a half. Somewhere behind is the OTRACO boat slowly overtaking us.

Eleven, still raining. Bestow for cargo. Three old boats, two upturned, on a tiny beach and two women sheltering under one from the rain. The passengers come down from the bush. The OTRACO boat overtakes us – thank goodness I'm not on it. The only place for a first-class passenger to sit, apart from his tiny cabin, is a few square feet of deck above the engines and very hot. One Congolais huddles there now. The waiting passengers shelter themselves under the big leaves of plantains. We have to retire and make room for OTRACO. The cargo here being very small and uncertain we go on to Bokoka for fear the cargoes there might be whipped up by OTRACO.

The three goats in the bow: the little one who is butted backwards and forwards between the others.

Monsieur Gourmont, a young planter at Bokabu, who had his first holiday in Europe after twelve years. Two daughters in Belgium, two small sons with him and a baby in his home. Brought a copy of *The Power and the Glory* for me to sign.*

* I only mentioned those books of mine because to an author there is a certain romance when stray copies of his work turn up in far, poor or abandoned places of the world. The European or American bookshelf gives no such gratification.

Quotation: The doctor said, 'He was what I would call a burnt-out case. There was no contagion left. If we had tests for minds as we have for leprosy the results would have been negative. He was mutilated of course and we don't spend time and money in arranging for these people occupational therapy (one knows how the sisters have taught Gratias Dei to knit sweaters even though he has no fingers). All the same I think this man had found his own, until these fools – these interfering fools . . .'

'Aren't you a little hard on the woman?' the youngest priest asked.

'Am I? She's the proudest woman in town. And the happiest. I feel tempted to tell her about the letters, they would be a disappointment to her, but then after all my business is only with the lepers.'

Wrote the above final sentences in the middle of the night. I wonder whether I shall ever reach them.* The book is changing out of all knowledge. The doctor now is not directly concerned: a bitter commentator. It is a plantation manager, a *colon*, jealous and stupid, his wife, pretty and stupid, who bring on the disaster to C.

How few letters there are one can use in place of a name. K belongs to Kafka, D I have used, X is self-conscious. There remains C. Can I avoid names altogether for the principals as I did in *The Power and the Glory*?†

---

* 'These fools – these interfering fools' was almost the only surviving phrase on the last page of the book.

†I don't know why X had so suddenly become C; if I was to avoid the national pinpointing which goes with surnames, C was the only initial that struck me as possible, since I had already used D in *The Confidential Agent*. Why all the other twenty-two letters were rejected, I don't know: C somehow had the only quality possible.

'The doctor looked at C with astonishment: the man had actually perpetrated a joke.'

February 23rd, on the River

A cool day so far. Still a bad throat and some rheumatism. Somebody last night left on board a copy of *Orient Express* for me to sign. We lay at Wakao. The *colon* we were expecting on board was ill with fever. Woken in the night by the noisy arrival of the OTRACO boat, and then kept awake by animal noises from the hens, cocks, goats.

Dreamt that I was concerned in some kind of Red Indian war. We were supposed to leave the Indians in peace for the night, but the men on guard had shot and killed one, so an attack was expected. I loaded two revolvers of an old-fashioned kind and felt an odd confidence and peace.*

Back to Lusaka and the madman waving the ship on with the help of a looking-glass. Then after lunch Imbonga and the same mission. Oh, how quickly tired one gets with the company of acquaintances. I long to be with friends again. But nearly three weeks must still pass.

The OTRACO boat catches us up before bed at Imbonga. It had run on the same snag and injured two propellers.

---

* The interest I always feel in dreams, not only my own dreams but the dreams of my characters, is probably the result of having been psycho-analysed at the age of sixteen. Querry's dream in *A Burnt-Out Case*, dealing with a lost priesthood and the search for sacramental wine, is an exact reproduction of one of my own dreams which occurred while I was writing the novel at the precise moment when I needed it. I wrote it in the next morning. My novel, *It's a Battlefield*, had its origin in a dream.

February 24th, on the River

Just another day of 421 and 'jollity' and killing flies.
Arrived at Flandria around nine and L. met the boat.
After beer on board sat up till nearly midnight drinking
whisky at his house in the sheer pleasure of talking English
to two intelligent people again.

February 25th, Flandria

A wet day and read and talked and drank till after
midnight: an orgy of pleasant social life.

February 26th, Yonda

Off by car with Father Jules. Stopped on the way – against
my will – to see a young administrator who paints pictures
– not very well – and has published a volume of verse.
Arrived at Yonda at midday and it was nice to run at once
into the Lechats and have lunch with them – like coming
home. He had obtained his new mattresses for the hospital,
but the day after they were installed he found the patients
lying on the floor. They told him that the sister had told
them they couldn't lie all day on the mattresses or they
would wear them out.

An enormous mail and piles of newspapers.
Father Henri turned up in the evening. Dinner and the
old routine with the fathers, and Father Henri and I

introduced the Superior and Brother Joseph to the delights of 421.

A commission on leprosy to meet in Coquilhatville under the honorary presidency of the Governor. It will consist of the local chief and a nurse who has had no experience of leprosy. No one invited from Yonda.

February 27th, Yonda

The old routine except that I no longer bother to go to the Congo to read.

Shopped in Coq and bought some native cottons, and a bottle of champagne for Madame Lechat.

Lechat spoke to me about one nun he had remarkable for her beauty. She was of good birth, family of means, with a university education. He said, 'I prefer a sister with some failings. She had none.' I asked whether she was a leprophil. No, he said, she would have been equally content to go anywhere and do anything under obedience. Completely efficient too. You could almost tell that from her hands on the steering wheel of the bus. Absolutely free from sentimentality.

Reading of a leproserie in French Guiana where the lepers are nearly all old convicts and of a strange man who helps in another leproserie not far away who is a burnt-out case psychologically – my C in fact. It is far in the wilds and one has to hire a plane and a jeep to reach it. Founded by

Mère Javoskey whose life has been written by Georges
Goyau.*

Purchases of equipment for the leproserie. In the
catalogue Father Pierre sees a picture of a bidet unknown
to him previously. He sees it as the ideal foot-bath for
ulcers and wants to order twelve, telephoning to Coq on
the matter. It had to be explained to him that a bidet has
other uses.

February 28th, Yonda

Visited the leprosy dispensary and completely empty
hospital in Coq. A contrast to Yonda, for here there is
everything and not a single in-patient.† But my main purpose was to meet the *dispensaire*, Mademoiselle Andre de
Jongh, GM, a war heroine who was said to have smuggled
nearly a thousand allied airmen out of Belgium before she
was arrested by the Germans and sent to a concentration
camp. She still looks young, though she must be over
forty, with humorous pretty eyes. She said she had picked
up her accent from having had as English teachers all the
British Commonwealth – Canadian, Australian, English.
She is reputed to have a wild but quickly burnt-out temper,

* I was tempted to delay my book and to visit French Guiana in case it
offered a better *mise-en-scène*, but I realized I would have to stay far
longer in an unfamiliar region. Indo-China had cost me four visits which
I could only afford by acting as a correspondent, and now I had chosen
Africa for the reason that I was already fairly familiar with the West,
after three months in Liberia before the war, and fifteen months in
Nigeria and Sierra Leone during the war – Negro Africa whether west or
central has much in common.

† This was because the hospital at Coq dealt only with the non-
contagious tuberculoid cases. All contagious cases were sent to Yonda.

and a book has been written about her by an Englishman, Airey Neave, called in French *Petit Cyclone*.*

The vegetation floating down the Congo a serious threat to navigation. The army is engaged in destroying it by poison, and the poison used is said after a time sometimes to send a man mad.

Evening drive with the doctor round a plantation and afterwards in vain search for hippos, to a village, Ikonga, to watch the sun set spectacularly across the Congo. Single *pirogues* pass across its path returning from fishing.

The deep blue-green of the palm plantation: ferns growing out of the pineapple-like bark.

After dinner went out with L. and Roland Wery, a police officer, round the African bars till two in the morning.† Polar beer advertisements. White jockey caps carrying the name Polar. The public women – lipsticks that take a mauve tint on an African mouth, and skin under make-up looks grey as though plastered with mourning clay. An old madman with his torn shirt and woman's handbag. A huge dispute outside the last bar because a woman had drunk the beer in a man's glass. The two women who solicited: 'There is lots of gonorrhoea and syphilis. We are safe.' The young debater in a bar – the thin fine hands of

* The doctor of the hospital who imagined that I was interested in his empty wards treated her like any subordinate: sending her to fetch cups of tea for us and allowing her no opportunity to join the conversation. I asked L. when we got home to invite her to Yonda.

† This was regarded by some of the white inhabitants of Coq as a wild folly.

Africans. He questioned the good faith of Europeans but was confused when I introduced Ghana. No real news of the world for the African. One felt in him an element of trust in the sincerity of our white argument, and yet the fear and confusion because he did not wish to disbelieve his own dogmatic theories. Another man might not have listened.

Back with Wery for a whisky. He praised my character of Scobie as an accurate representation of a colonial police officer.* Home at 2.45 and tomorrow's expedition to a lake cancelled.

Remember: Injections are the same medicine as DDS conveyed in oil to slow the effect. They are an alternative to the tablets, more expensive and taken less frequently. Query once a month? The doctor now gives two tablets two or three times a week, not daily, and there is no need for a monthly intermission. He intermits only at such times as are convenient. The sister's annual retreat, etc. Vitamin tablets (B.12?) were given as at Imbonga because it was believed that DDS caused anaemia, but the doctor now believes the cause to be such complaints as hookworms. 'It is cheaper to give them lavatories.'

The town councillor at Ikonga seeks work but can't get

* I was pleased with his praise as one is always pleased by professional approval – all the more in this case as the character had been attacked by George Orwell with his experience of the Burma Police as impossibly humane for a Commissioner of Colonial police. But I had worked fairly closely with an old Commissioner in Freetown and I knew his affection for the African and the depth of his sympathy. His humanity took one bizarre form – after a hanging at which he had to be present he could not eat meat for a fortnight (this spoilt for him the Christmas of 1942).

any because of his illiteracy. The other councillors say he is a bad man – he can only have been elected because he is a witch-doctor and made a medicine (from the bark of trees, etc.). The witch with the red bark make-up carrying a bell outside the market.

Stories of a Père Georges* who was found drowned recently. Georges did nothing at all at the mission but say Mass. The rest of the time he spent hunting and collecting specimens of wild birds for a museum (he had his own *pirogue*). But at the same time he had a close relation with the Africans, talking to them as he went here and there, and when his body was brought back to the mission, the Africans lined the road and knelt as his body passed.

March 1st, Sunday, Yonda

The doctor in the novel: 'Occasionally he became conscious of the smell of the Africans around his table, and his heart moved quickly as it had done on his first day in Africa.'†

Hangover: stayed in bed till nearly eight: cup of coffee: lunch with the fathers: a long siesta: reading *The Wilder Shores of Love* – a terribly over-written book: down into Coq with L. and a beer at the smaller restaurant. Mass in Coq (of a most unreligious kind): everybody turning their chairs and themselves as in a dance, so that one felt a partner of the woman in front. Most unattractive colonial

* Not the captain of the boat.
† A sentence which does not seem to have been used in the book.

types. The usual low benches a few inches high for the African.

Discrimination has taken a turn the other way. The white man pays more than the black for his radio licence: in the courts unless there are witnesses the word of the black, say that a white man has struck him, is always taken against the white's, which leads to a kind of blackmail. The masochism of Europe – many nuns received letters from Europe on learning the events in Leopoldville – 'We have brought it on ourselves.' No realization of the work selflessly done for the Africans.

The bustles of the black women: these partly caused by a kind of rope of plastic rings they wear round their hips next to the skin. The richer they are, the more their rings. The sexual significance. Do they wear them during intercourse?

Birth control here not the problem. The African a dying race owing to the sterility of the women due to gonorrhoea. The doctor recently had a girl of eight with gonorrhoea.

March 2nd, Yonda

Within limits of abnormality, every individual loves himself. In cases where he has a deformity or abnormality or develops it later, his own aesthetic sense revolts and he develops a sort of disgust towards himself. Though with time, he becomes reconciled to his deformities, it is only on the conscious level. His subconscious mind, which continues to bear the mark of the injury, brings about certain changes in his whole personality, making him suspicious of society. Even if we strip leprosy of all its stigma, a leprosy patient will develop all these complexes arising out of the disfigurement. R. V. Wardekar.*

Père J. speaks of a row which started between one of the *infirmiers* and his wife at 5.30 this morning. These rows can often be heard all round one at any hour of the night. They are partly the result of a virtual enslavement of women. A secondary education has only been started for girls in the last few years. An educated African can find no woman of equal education to marry. But the resentment of the slave imposes also a kind of slavery on the man. As the woman does the heavy work she can make life very unsupportable for her master.

The dispensary: the burnt-out cases: no toes on one foot, two on the other: both thumbs gone. Treatment for psychological reasons only.

Paraffin wax baths for palsy: temperatures must be just right – patient cannot feel the heat owing to atrophied nerves. Danger of fire. Wax used over and over again because of expense.

The child brought in with fever. The doctor exposes on the breast the mark of where a knife has been used to cut the skin and insert native medicine. He is angry with the woman and she puts the blame on the grandmother.

Palsy of the eyes: can be treated by having the eyelids stitched up, but the patients often refuse.

Back to dispensary after short siesta: the man who had

* This quotation from an essay I read at Yonda in the doctor's library provided me with an epigraph for *A Burnt-Out Case.*

had leprosy in the testicles and one breast dangled like a woman's. He was being treated very satisfactorily with 1906, but the sweet baked smell of sloughed leprous skin filled the dispensary.

In the evening Mademoiselle de Jongh and a friend in for drinks. Quite ready to talk about her war experiences and much came out that was not in the book. She and her organization were betrayed by two American pilots who were told by the Germans that they would be shot as spies if they did not prove they were officers by reconstructing every stage of their journey from Belgium to the Pyrenees.* Americans in general she found very lack-lustre in escaping: they all thought there must be some easier way of getting to Spain than on their feet; none of them knew how to walk. (She said the Americans would tell her that it was impossible to go further: the British that they were very tired but would go on till they could go no further – which never happened. The same complaint applied to Canadians. She obviously preferred the British. Her two

* Miss de Jongh, then in her early twenties, turned up at the British Consulate in San Sebastian after the fall of France with two allied civilians whom she had escorted from Brussels and asked the consul for money to establish an escape route. He suspected a German plant and told her that he was only interested in allied airmen. After a few months she returned with two pilots who had been shot down over Belgium. She had enlisted the aid of a *contrebandier* in the Pyrenees, but before the last journey he went down with flu and while she and three airmen (two American and one British) were holed up in a farm-house waiting for his recovery they were spotted by Vichy police. She owed her life to the fact that she was handed over under an assumed name to the German Air Force police who did not realize that she was the notorious de Jongh for whom the Gestapo were searching. As a result of the American betrayal the whole escape route was destroyed, several people were executed including her own father, and more than a hundred went to concentration camps.

73

worst escapees, however, were Belgians who had to be carried two hours at a time by her *contrebandier*.)

The characters Geoff (Australian) and Jim (British) who had a friendly bickering rivalry. Jim was wounded and G. insisted that he jump first. He hadn't fastened his parachute properly and it was whirling away from him when he caught it with one hand. Jim was baby-faced and Geoff tough. Geoff carried Jim and said that never again would he carry an Englishman. Jim said that he would never allow himself again to be carried by an Australian. A doctor at an address they had been given in England gave Jim an injection which he said would enable him to walk the two miles to Waterloo. But at Waterloo they were given bicycles and told to go straight on to Brussels. At Brussels two railway tickets intended for two men who had been captured were ready for that night, so poor Jim had to be off again. The guide was told to take a camp-stool and see that the wounded man sat on it if the train were crowded, but as Geoff had got a burn on his face the guide thought that he was the wounded man and made him take the seat. Neither Geoff nor Jim could speak French so that they couldn't put the mistake right, and every time Geoff tried to give up his seat he was ordered down on to it again. Only in Paris outside the station when Jim fainted did the guide understand his mistake. Within a week of being shot down they were back in England and Geoff was killed on his next sortie.

She spoke as though all had been a joke and the years happy years – only once did she refer to nervous strain. She was funny even about the concentration camp where each

74

five people were allotted so little space for sleeping that they had to fit themselves sideways and when one turned all turned. One night she heard a very middle-class Brussels voice complaining indignantly about her, 'Look at her. Sleeping on her back like a queen.'

The noise of insects outside the doctor's house as we talked: 'There is never any silence in the Congo, except for an hour in the afternoon when it is too hot to enjoy it.' Then she spoke of the wonderful silence of the Pyrenees at night.*

I asked her why she had come to the Congo. 'Because from the age of fifteen I wanted to cure the lepers. If I had delayed any longer it would have been too late.'

She became a Catholic in 1947.

March 3rd, Yonda

DDS sometimes has the effect of making a patient temporarily mad. The patient who asked to have his hands bound because of his desire to attack people. 'I told him,' the doctor said, 'that at eight o'clock you will feel worse. At eleven o'clock worse, but a few more hours and you will feel as you do now, and after that less....' The patient was able to hold on.

The new ointment which has a very quick effect: there have been cures in a few months: but so abominable a smell that it makes people sick. The cures have to be reinforced of course with DDS.

* German patrols could always be heard a long way off by the noise their boots made.

The man without toes and with one testicle the size of a croquet ball who cohabits with an ex-polio patient who has tiny paralysed legs and can only crawl. They have a healthy child. He is a Catholic catechist.

The man with no nose, a terrible claw hand and mutilated feet.

The child from the bush who lost a toe from jiggers.

Lepromine used to determine the resistance of an undetermined patient to see which course the disease will take.

March 4th, Yonda

Tomorrow start for home. The doctor after reading *La Gana* has a bad night and dreams we all have an accident in the car.

Felt a bit tired with sun, and atmosphere very heavy. Duty drinks with the Governor and his wife. Then with them to the burgomaster and his wife to sign their Golden Book, bought a bottle of champagne and relaxed with the L.'s.

March 5th

A quiet morning, spinning out *The Path to Rome* which I don't dislike as much as when I was a boy (it is more forgivable than the *Voyage of the Nona*, for Belloc was a young man who may be allowed to cut a dash): I have to be careful, since I am running short of books.

The number of bicycles possessed by the young Africans.

They are stacked outside the dispensary as they are stacked outside a Cambridge college.

Arrived Leopoldville. Met at terminus by M. who took me to hotel. The longed-for bath, disturbed only by two telephone calls and a written message.

March 6th, Leopoldville

Usual trouble with a journalist. Made an appointment for tomorrow evening when I shall be gone.

Oh, the would-be writers. Out to drinks with a tired man who had once written me a fan letter about his son and *The Little Train*. Married to the third most attractive woman I've seen in the Congo. Driving me back to the hotel he opened, as they say, his heart. It was his ambition to write – something 'creative' if only a page or two, but now he was tired, sick and middle-aged.

March 7th, Brazzaville

Forced to give the interview I thought I was going to dodge, and caught a boat at 9.30. The tiny little port of Leo with a ticket kiosk, a *douane* who looked only at the baggage of Africans, and a white immigration officer who attended only whites. On the opposite side all officials black and no examination even for whites. What opportunities today for a white smuggler between African territories.

Brazzaville a far prettier, more sympathetic place than Leo – Europe in Leo weighs down on the African soil in the form of skyscrapers: here Europe sinks into the greenery and trees of Africa. Even the shops have more chic than Leo. The inhabitants of Leo call this a village, but at least it is a charming provincial village and not a dull city.

Quiet day. Took a taxi in the evening to a bookshop and bought the first volume of *The Complete Goncourt Journals*. Whisky by myself in my room. It was nice, for a while, being alone.

Hinduism is a tropical religion: a reaction from indiscriminate slaughter, which only happens in the tropics. For every insect one kills in Europe, one must kill a hundred at least in tropical countries. One kills without thinking – a smear on one's napkin or on the pages of one's book.

Gave myself a good dinner and perhaps that caused a bad night which followed.

Possible epigraph: 'There are doorways and dust-heaps for such deaths, and such despair.' Dickens.

March 8th, Brazzaville

Finishing *David Copperfield*. Is a picture missing or is my memory wrong? Surely there was once a picture of Steerforth on the wreck, or was the picture in my mind only? Steerforth always attracted me, and just as when a child I was stirred by Mr Murdstone and his cane, perhaps the death of Steerforth helped to fix in me my fear of death by drowning.

The court of the hotel is haunted by poor young Africans whom some wretched European artist has taught to turn out 'decorative' pictures of dancers on black paper – all the same designs. I suppose they sell some to tourists. This artist was admired by the librarian in Leo who proudly showed me one of his pictures – no better, no worse, in fact indistinguishable except in size, from these pictures by the students of his atelier. When one compares what he has done here with the genuine art movement started by an American in Haiti, one is appalled at the waste and corruption.

I wonder who it was reading David Ogg's *England in the Seventeenth Century* in Brazzaville airport?

English papers of March 7th on the plane. How?
Libreville: pretty little airport all trees and water like a country railway station. Back in the West in sight of the Atlantic. A big party going on to see an African off to Paris. Complete mixing, not only of black and white, but men and women. Contrast here to Belgian Congo where women are still uneducated. A black priest. Black girls – very pretty ones in European clothes and short balloon skirts. Too great a cordiality and shaking of hands and noisy affability. Colonialism in hurried and undignified retreat. Compare the official retreat in Belgian Congo and the orders to officials not to 'tutoyer'. But one had the feeling all the same of the worst whites mixing with the worst blacks. Nearly everybody drinking whisky at 4.30 in the afternoon. The stringy wet sweaty hair of white women.
At Douala met by B., an old friend from Indo-China.

Drinks with him and an American in the bar, and then with B. to my hotel. A genuinely air-conditioned room with a lovely view of palms, forest and water. In the evening sense of pretty, well-dressed women, with good make-up, dancing, gaiety, unknown in an English colony. With B. and another man to the Frégate – black prostitutes and a tiny dance floor. Young French sailors standing drinks and dancing with the prostitutes cheek by cheek. One girl of great beauty with sad and humane eyes.

TWO
CONVOY TO WEST AFRICA

Breakfast in the Adelphi at Liverpool – the huge solid over-grown pub: the sense of comfort and security and being on dry land. Then a taxi-drive through battered streets to the dock, tearing up letters which hadn't been sealed by the censor and scattering them through the window. Empty Sabbath-like wastes with nobody about to ask the way. The difficulty of finding something as large as a ship. At last the ship – a small, 5,000-ton oil-driven cargo ship, one of the newest of the Elder Dempsters, with neat bright little single-berth cabins and only twelve passengers. Three RNVR officers (one had only been twice at sea in his life as far as Hamburg): some Fleet Air Arm petty officers; an elderly American civilian, Professor Whittemore, a great authority on Byzantine art and a vegetarian: two oil-men: an odd foreigner with very little English, a great square head and the strangest square plus-fours. About 2.30 we start. A last look at England in Mersey mist, but then the positively last appearance doesn't come off: we anchor in the Mersey. After tea boat-drill – the rather boisterous occasion which used to turn up once on every sea voyage: this time a serious rehearsal. Nobody enjoys it much. All day two rafts are suspended on a slope each side of the ship ready to be cut loose: one hold contains rubber rafts. On the poop the anti-aircraft men in khaki and any old sweater keep watch round the Bofors gun.

After dinner one of the RNVR officers, middle-aged with a Glasgow accent, tries heartily to pull us together. We 'volunteer' for submarine and machine-gun watches.

We are making for Belfast tomorrow and the odd
foreigner is a Dutchman – one collects scraps of information, just as in the old days on the first evening of a cruise.
One establishes a home with the scraps. . . . The second
officer has been twice blown up.

I unpack my books and then pack them up again after
looking at the new covers. I talk to Sparks. He has been
away from the sea for ten years in a radio business of his
own. He has returned unenthusiastically to escape the
army. Everybody in the ship from the captain to the
kitchen hands seems new to her. They wander round
finding their way about like the passengers.

Began reading *The Mask of Dimitrios*, by Eric Ambler.
Visiting a stranger's flat one always looks at the bookcases.
Whittemore has on board Rowse's *Tudor Cornwall*,
Huxley's *Grey Eminence*, Laurence Binyon's poems; F.,
the young RNVR officer who seems likely to prove my
drinking companion, has brought *The Pickwick Papers*.
There is a tiny library in the smoking-room but it isn't open
yet.

'We'll get properly organized,' the Glasgow man says,
'tomorrow.'

Tonight one will sleep safely quiet in the Mersey.

10 December

We leave after breakfast. Passengers are to man three
four-hour watches during the day: two men on machine-

guns above the boat deck for aircraft, and two below the
bridge for submarines. The Glasgow man is head of my
watch. One climbs a short vertical steel ladder into a kind
of conning tower containing each a gun with steel shield. A
sailor shows us how to tilt the gun and fire: he is one of the
few who were in this ship last trip. Two ships were
torpedoed the first night out from the Mersey, but the
passengers' watches had only continued two days. The
submarine watchers had watched from the bridge, but they
had got so drunk the captain had refused to allow them
there again. Little fear of that this time – we are a very
sober, sedate company. The siren keeps on blowing –
rather disturbing as one must count the blasts – seven short
and a long for boat stations.

A cold grey day: the sea getting up: soldiers in Bala-
clavas by the Bofors: a black steward making water in the
bilge.

Two hours watch, and a half an hour as well relieving the
previous watch for lunch. Then an hour on submarine
watch – bitter cold especially to port. Even a bird can look
like a periscope. At dinner the Chief told us that in weather
like this it was easy for a submarine to follow a ship un-
observed during the day above water and submerge at
night for the attack. Two ships in which he had served had
been torpedoed after he had left them. One hopes that his
luck will hold. Never more than five days' leave between
voyages.

An hour with the machine-gun – a little less cold up

there. The steel shields like the wings of black angels. Past the Isle of Man, and a plane in the sky, presumably one of ours. News on the wireless of the sinking by the Japs of the *Prince of Wales* and the *Repulse*.

It's odd how on submarine duty one thinks only of that danger and on machine-gun duty only of the air. Perched up above the deck one hears the wind in the wires like choral singing from inside a church.

Felt seasick at tea and lay down till dinner. In the bitter cold of the bows recited Hail Marys to distract myself. Over and over again one forgets that this is war, looking forward to the south and the warm weather, then the sense of danger comes back like nausea. I wear a vest at night, only partly for the sake of warmth. About midnight the siren woke me. I counted seven short blasts and in the hurry of getting out of bed I didn't notice the fact that there was no long blast. Wondered bemusedly what to put on first. Then the quiet made me hesitate and think. My next-door neighbour was less cautious. I saw a Fleet Air Arm uniform flash past the door, and then I saw him return slowly. We are all new boys who don't know the customs. It was only the approach to Belfast. After a day at sea the curious effect of voices shouting *outside* the ship: the odd casualness of, 'Do you want a pilot?'

11 December

Lying in the lough outside Belfast.

The Fleet Air Arm warrant officers cling together: they

are distinguished from officers by the extravagant cleanness of their shirts and collars: they wear gloves all
day.

Books for a desert island – this is what I have brought
with me for the Coast. Short notice prevented me getting
Gibbon and *Anna Karenina*.

Short Stories of De Maupassant
The Old Testament (in the World's Classics)
The New Testament and *Acts* (in the World's Classics)
Father and Son, by Edmund Gosse
The Mask of Dimitrios, by Ambler
Wanderings in South America, by Waterton
The Knapsack, Herbert Read's anthology
Oxford Book of Seventeenth Century Verse
Selected Poems of Rilke
Selected Poems of Wordsworth
Golden Treasury
Broadway Book of English Verse
Penguin Selection of Browning
Blackwell's one-volume Shakespeare
Kindness in a Corner, by T. F. Powys
Life of Tolstoy, by Aylmer Maude
North and South, by Mrs Gaskell
Haydon's *Autobiography*

and a number of Trollope's – *The Duke's Children, Can
You Forgive Her?, Ayala's Angel, Ralph the Heir, The
American Ambassador, Sir Harry Hotspur*, and *Miss
Mackenzie*.

So far in spite of nausea and watches I have kept up an average of 500 words a day on British Dramatists.*

All day hove to in the lough. The Dutchman turns out to be a Pole born in Georgia who fought in the Russian army during the last war: a Mahommedan. He explains something with a map to Whittemore: the square monolithic face becomes suddenly kindly because at last he can communicate in his own language. Whittemore seems to know all languages. An elderly man with an old maid's face and feminine wrinkles and steel spectacles and an extraordinary gentleness and kindness of manner. He has a flat in London and a house in Massachusetts where he was born which belonged to his great-grandfather. He also has a *pied-à-terre* in Istanbul.

At six listened to the wireless in the steward's cabin. Germany's declaration of war on America. Whittemore gently and courteously pleased. 'We are allies now.'

The ship's library open. Read Hanley's *The Ocean* – an open-boat story. It seemed unreal. No mention of the Cold.

Found an old acquaintance in the purser, who had been in the *David Livingstone* when I went to Liberia years ago.

Books in the chief steward's cabin included a Dunsany, Silone's *Fontamara* and Mottram's *Spanish Farm*.

* A short book I had been commissioned to write for a series called *Britain in Pictures* – long out of print.

12 December

Into Belfast. Little white lighthouses on stilts: a buoy that seems to have a table tied to it: a sunken ship right up in the dock. Cranes like skeleton foliage in a steely winter. The flicker of green flame in the bellies of building ships. Hundreds of dock-yard workers stop altogether to see one small ship come in.

Endless impatient waiting for the immigration officer to come on board. Why the anxiety to get ashore in so dull a place? It is the cruise-spirit perhaps. I thought it just as well to go to Confession before the Atlantic. The hideous Catholic church difficult to find in Protestant Belfast. At the Presbytery a tousled housekeeper tried to send me away when I asked for a confession. 'This is no time for confession,' trying to shut the door in my face.* The dreadful parlour hung with pious pictures as unlived in as a dentist's waiting-room, and then the quiet, nice young priest who called me 'son' and whose understanding was of the simplest.† In the same street the pious repository selling Woodbines from under the counter to old women.

In the evening a dozen and a half Galway oysters and a pint and a half of draught Guinness at the Globe. Then back to the ship. W. had lunched with the Consul-General.

* Years later this incident cropped up again in my second play *The Potting Shed.*

† He did seem to me, however, unnecessarily curious about the convoy.

'The last time I saw him,' he said gently, 'was on the military road they were building in Georgia to Tiflis.'

'Glasgow' turns out to be the drunk one traditionally has on board every West Coast boat. He had been on shore to see the dentist and he showed us two gaps where teeth had been drawn. 'When the captain heard that,' said the chief steward, 'he said, "I've never heard that one before. Soap and matches is what the sailors say when they want to go ashore for a woman."'

'Glasgow' with his little hooked bird's nose and his sudden tipsy release of mental activity was like a minor prophet. You felt he was the chief character in a play like *Outward Bound*, the chorus who warns the audience that the ship is doomed. 'Well, gentlemen,' he had us all penned in the small smoking room, 'we're going to be to-gether for five or six weeks, and there's going to be a wonderful interchange of mind. I've been looking forward to this, the wonderful discussions we'll have. We've come into this ship all thinking different things, but when we go out of that door we'll all think the same. Discussions – I don't like argument. Discussions. Political discussions. I'm not interested in what *you* think: I'm interested in what I think. We'll knit it all up together. This is a wonderful experience. It will be the most wonderful experience of my life, the deepest experience. I'll impose on you all what I think. I won't disguise it from you, gentlemen, I'm a drinker. I buried my wife last August and since then poor Joe's had nothing to do but get drunk. A clean break. I look forward, gentlemen, to the wonderful discussions we'll have. I'll learn – it's the only thing worth doing, learning. I shan't learn a lot: I shall learn a little bit. But somebody said a book is worth reading if you only learn from one sentence. I couldn't remember these quotations if I wasn't drunk.' The unwinking gentle courtesy of W. as this went on. 'Glasgow' has certainly succeeded in transforming the dead sobriety of the ship since the first day. It is more like the old *David Livingstone*.

The chief steward gave advice. Always leave one's door hooked ajar. After leaving Belfast always sleep in trousers, shirt and pullover: you don't bother to dress properly in an emergency with the lights out. He prefers a submarine attack to a plane: usually more time to abandon ship. He was torpedoed his last trip and they had three-quarters of an hour. Only one man killed in the engine-room.

The Pole argued about religion when 'Glasgow' had staggered to bed. 'I am Mussulman.' He demonstrated with glasses. 'This one is Negro, this is Catholic, this is Protestant, this is Mussulman. All same God.' His objection to English draughts (at which he is beaten) as compared with Continental. 'It is not strong. No strategy.' He abandons the game in despair.

13 December

We leave Belfast. Again the showers of sparks from the oxyacetylene welders and the blue and green lights of the electric welders. The open hull of an aircraft-carrier lights up like a toy stage as a welder gets to work and a tiny figure can be seen against the confused background of steel – then darkness again and then again the green light and the tiny figure.

We lie all day in the lough. The captain goes off in a launch for orders. Rumour that we shall be here three days. Perhaps a dozen cargo-ships smaller than ours lie around, a destroyer, a merchant cruiser with a plane on board painted blue and white, and a beautiful windy little corvette hung with bunting like a Picasso water-colour which steams round the ships in the late afternoon as though to take a look at her charges. An impression that departure is near.

At 4.30 p.m. boat-drill. Distribution of small red-globed electric torches which clip on the shoulder and help one to be observed in the water.

After dinner 'Glasgow' comes into the smoking room drunk again. He has his wish and involved us all in argument by dropping the statement: 'Winston. I've got no use for him. A political adventurer. Tell me one success he's had.' I think old W. was shocked – perhaps more shocked by the equanimity of the other passengers. Before 'Glasgow' arrived he had been dropping gentle and random remarks – the best restaurant in Cairo: how they make coffee in the Caucasus: a sweet-scented night flower in India, sitting there in a disreputable old soft hat and a scarf twisted round the neck (the scarf I think came from Albania). 'Glasgow' began to argue hotly in favour of dictatorship against democracy, and suddenly W. dropped softly, 'I have a letter Abraham Lincoln wrote to my grandfather. My grandfather was angry with him for not passing quickly an anti-slavery law. Lincoln's last sentence was – ' W.'s voice became a soft, poetic croon: '"The people must decide or how are we greater than Kings?" '

The fourth engineer has skipped the ship and will presumably try to get across to Eire. He was ten pounds in the company's debt and couldn't get a drink till it was paid off. How oddly dramatic ships are. My last voyage – in a German ship from Vera Cruz – the cook committed suicide rather than return home. That was in 1938. The ships around us are not part of the convoy. Tomorrow morning we start for the rendezvous, but if there's a fog we may miss it and have to wait weeks for another.

14 December

A rough day between 9 and 4 and a little before tea I was sick. Unable to write. We leave the lough and join a line of about seven ships. Submarine watch 9 to 10.15: with the machine-gun 10.15 to 11.30, and then after a rather scanty lunch relieved someone at the gun from 1 to 1.30. The last watch high wind and icy sleet. Couldn't get warm afterwards. Lay down. By teatime we were in calmer water coming up by Bute towards Greenock, presumably to meet the rest of the convoy. Bright brown heather on one side and a wild sunset blazing up behind the hills on the other. Sunset reflected on the seagull's wings. We drop anchor and wait. Manage to do a little work on *British Dramatists*. Anyway one more night in safety and pyjamas. Happidrome is blazing out from the radio in the steward's cabin: shouts of comedians and blares of mechanical laughter. Left again at midnight. Read *Herr Witch Doctor*, by Sarah Gertrude Millin.

15 and 16 December

Rough both days. Making no more than 4 knots against a head-wind going south-west. Sick both days. During the afternoon watch on Tuesday, a plane came low over the convoy, and another ship fired a machine-gun at it. It was one of our planes, but the gunner was technically correct. Our planes are not allowed to fly directly over a convoy. No writing either day. Old W. has brought a supply of Ovaltine with him and has it last thing at night.

18 December

Stormy again after one fine day. Party began in the chief steward's room at 10 a.m. and continued till I went on duty at 12.30. The second engineer played the piano, the purser tried to sing, and the second steward served what he called 3d. cocktails – rum and milk – giving a dramatic recitation in a tin hat.

After lunch quiet reigned and old W. talked gently of Henry James and his brother William, and the box he had shared with Henry and the Ranee of Sarawak at the disastrous first night of *Guy Domville*.* The submarine

* I am sure he told me this, but, according to Mr Leon Edel, James did not attend the first night, but only arrived in the wings after the fall of the curtain.

watch has been abolished as we are on the inside of the convoy.

The chief steward tells me he is nervous at night: this is his first trip after being torpedoed and his cabin looks exactly like the previous one. The second steward, who is a little cracked, has been torpedoed three times, but the gipsy told him he wouldn't be torpedoed a fourth. W. tells an anecdote of Gertrude Stein, who was asked at a lecture why it was that she answered questions so clearly and wrote so obscurely. 'If Keats was asked a question would you expect him to reply with the Ode to a Grecian Urn?'

19 December

The second steward – the cracked one – was a prisoner for two years in the last war – according to him in Siberia. I don't know how this works out. He explains his paunch by it. 'I hate them,' he says, blocking the way in his white jacket. 'I'd kill a German child that high. I'd kill a German woman who was pregnant with one. If I'm alive you'll hear of me after the war in Lord Beaverbrook's papers. I might have gone into Parliament after the last war if I'd chosen. And if I die, I've left a letter for my two daughters – they'll carry on. There'll be two rebels in England if they try to let them off this time.'

'Don't talk of dying.'

'I'll never die. I live by prayer, I pray at sunrise and sunset like a Mahommedan.' (He is a Catholic.)

All the time he and the chief steward are immensely stirred and excited by the idea of Christmas.

The second waylays the passengers and tries with bulky importance to arrange a Christmas entertainment. Huge plans are discussed and disappear again: the drink gamble (everybody to put in £2 and drink as much as they like), a treasure hunt for a bottle of whisky. Crowded meetings in the steward's cabin.

Today for an hour or two it was sunny and even warm, but now we've begun to roll again and the weather has clouded. Last night we were supposed to be about the latitude of Newcastle – ten days after going on board.

At night 'Glasgow' drunk and boring. 'I am drunk all the time. Drunk at breakfast. I've got a bottle of rum in my cabin. I'm drunk and proud of it. I hate criticism. Why shouldn't I be drunk? It feels good to be drunk and it sharpens the intellect.' The Fleet Air Arm warrant officers watch him disapprovingly, wearing gloves.

20 December

Rough again. Eleven days since we started and it's doubtful whether we are yet the latitude of Land's End.

Explosion in one ship at about 6 a.m. and a warning bell to the crew. Rumour now says we are parallel to Brest. A heavy swell, and on the last watch thick mist coming up.

21 December

Early watch with heavy mist – visibility about 100 yards

and ships' sirens all blowing different tones. About 8.15 the mist rose, and there we all still were in our exact places, chugging slowly on. A destroyer dropped depth-charges while we were at breakfast and later raced by towards the head of the convoy. For the first time we sat out all the morning drinking gin and vermouth. Apparently we carry a cargo of TNT as well as aeroplanes. The passengers become nervously humorous on the subject. By the evening we had altered course again to the west. Shall we never go south? A notice has been posted that we will not be served meals without lifebelts, which we must take everywhere. Shared a bottle of 1929 Beaune (5s.). There is a little pre-war store of wine on board. Claret at 3s. 6d. and champagne at 21s.

22 December

Colder again but about eight we turned south and after lunch some of the convoy turned off over the south-western horizon. We missed their presence.

The gunlayer, who was in the Post Office, shivering in his jersey: sad brown eyes: one of the only two naval men in the crew. He complained of the impossibility of getting covers for his guns which rust in the salt damp. The Elder Dempster offices, he said, full of young women making tea: 'They all seem to have plenty of tea and sugar.' Note how on a ship all the time people seem to be tying up things with string, balanced in reckless positions.

Finished *Parents and Children*, by Compton-Burnett,

disposed of Congreve in *British Dramatists*,* played three
games of chess with the Pole, winning one.

23 December

Drank with the chief steward. He feels very jittery at night.
Hasn't yet gone to bed but lies on his couch. The cargo of
depth-charges and TNT under his cabin.

Legend of foreign ships in convoys which deliberately
show lights to help the enemy. When this happens the
Commodore appoints a rendezvous, and the convoy
scatters. The foreign ship finds itself alone at the rendezvous: the rest of the convoy has taken a different course.

For the first time in the afternoon real warm sun and blue
sea. Played chess with the Pole. It is not to be avoided. If I
lie down in the afternoon he pokes his shaven Mongolian
head through the cabin door and says, 'Check?' During
the game he sings all the time to himself, 'Good. Very good.
It is very good,' and tries to take back his pieces. I won one
game in four.

24 December

Warmer and sunnier. Passing between the Azores in sight
of land. A party again with the steward, the purser and

* Was it the rough seas and cold watches that made me write so harshly
of Congreve? 'Poor despised Crowne, in *The Country Wit*, had provided
as good situations: Shadwell had had more life, and Wycherley more
stagecraft – Congreve like the smooth schoolboy stole the prize.'

'Glasgow' before lunch. The steward demonstrates how to test a French letter. Keeping the watch now from deck-chairs.

Started the evening with a half-bottle of champagne. Then Beaune for dinner followed by port and brandy. Then down to the stewards to help with Christmas decorations, developing into a party that only finished at 2.30 a.m. French letters blown up the size of balloons and hung over the captain's chair. The black steward Daniel stood on his hands and put his feet round his neck. The Fleet Air Arm sang 'Danny Boy', 'When Irish Eyes are Smiling', 'Widdecombe Fair' and the like. The cracked second steward became boring with over-repeated turns: we had heard so often already the poem in praise of the Merchant Service written by his daughter and recited for no apparent reason in a steel helmet. The chief steward put on a cloth cap and gave a dramatic recitation about a lamp-lighter. Then Cookie in his dirty white singlet and dirty white apron, thin consumptive fanatical face with long razor nose and three days' beard. He sang a magnificent anonymous ballad on the sinking of the Elder Dempster liner *Vestris* to a melancholy tune. He copied it out for me afterwards and this is how it went.

THE SINKING OF THE S.S. 'VESTRIS'

Proudly she sailed from New York City,
Bound for a land o'er the Sea,
And on her decks the wives and husbands,
Children with hearts gay and free.

She sailed on her way o'er the deep blue Ocean,
With never a thought or a fear,
But there on the Bridge stood Captain Carey,
A Sailor for many a year.

Then came the storm that hit the *Vestris*,
Wild waves were roaring high,
And there in her side a hole was poundered,
Then they knew that death was nigh.

Great was the toll of life that was taken,
Husbands and Wives torn apart,
Many a home with loved ones missing,
Many a sad broken heart.

There on the Bridge stood Captain Carey,
Hoping his Ship he could save,
But too late he sent a message,
The *Vestris* was doomed to her grave.

Sad were the cries of Men and Women,
Mothers with babes held so tight,
Brave men who fought to save their loved ones,
Lifeboats that sank in the night.

There on the deck stood a grey-haired Captain,
Waiting for death to befall,
Yet we know that someone blundered,
He must forgive after all.

We are all adrift on life's mighty Ocean,
Where each mistake has its cost,

And we must learn from this sad story,
He who hesitates is lost.

25 December

Christmas Day started at 11 in the morning with a bottle of champagne to cure the hangover. Round-the-Empire broadcast and the King's rather lugubrious speech at lunch. Dinner with a huge menu. Hors d'oeuvre, soup, fried whiting, tinned asparagus, roast turkey and chipolatas, plum pudding, grapefruit ice. It was like peace. Toasts to the King, Churchill, Roosevelt (for W.), Sikorski (for the Pole), etc. Then the captain, mate and the chief came to the smoking room. A shy RNVR officer tried to play hymns (the only tunes he knew), but the atmosphere by that time was not propitious. Played Sing, Say or Pay. Broke up traditionally at midnight with Auld Lang Syne, and afterwards I settled down to chess with the Pole. One was less homesick than one had expected. Presumably that was the drink. Woke up at about 5 in the morning with an explosion: I thought that one of the convoy had caught it, but it must have been the clap of the wind as we changed course.

26 December

Nothing to record but a slight somnolence. Even the convoy seemed a bit jaded. More rusty than ever and no bunting.

27 December

The chief steward depressed. On his last voyage he was

torpedoed just about here – nine days from Freetown. They lost seven ships in three nights – his ship was the last to go. One had forgotten there is such a thing as a straits in the Atlantic, but between Dakar and Freetown the coast juts out to meet the Brazilian bulge, and that Atlantic channel is the happy hunting-ground for submarines. Naturally every sailor is convinced that the submarines are using the port of Dakar whatever the politicians say.

It is warmer and sunnier. Reading Huxley's *Grey Eminence* with unexpected pleasure.

Third boat-drill this evening. Afterwards few people seemed to be about the deck though the evening was balmy. I don't know whether the tension is in my own mind alone, or among all the passengers.

28 December

My daughter's birthday. Drank champagne in her honour before lunch and split two bottles of claret at night. Party in chief steward's cabin afterwards. I feel now as if I'm just coming out from under an anaesthetic, and I feel scared of the loneliness I shall feel when I leave the ship. Have given up drinking gin – it's too depressing.

29 December

The heat is really being turned on now. Went very slow all day – presumably to keep a rendezvous. Nightmare at night of the traditional kind – being trapped in darkness.

30 December

The Commodore's ship breaks down and one escort ship remains behind with her. Rumour says we are about opposite Dakar.

Very hot in the afternoon. Read on deck. Agatha Christie's *Evil under the Sun* and Rilke. It was like a lazy day on a peacetime cruise. Over and over again one began to think it peace and this a holiday, and then one would remember that an explosion might come at any minute.

Party before lunch and before dinner in the steward's cabin. The usual West Coast tales are starting up like plants in the heat. How one remembers them from eight years back. The doctor who cuts a tumour off a black girl's breast and tosses it to her waiting relatives. 'Here's a dash.'

The black crew are partly paid in rice – so many tobacco tins a day. They insist on the tobacco tin as a measure, not realizing that it only needs a little pressure by the thumb on the bottom of the tin to reduce their ration by a tiny amount on each tin.

The flushed constipated Fleet Air Arm warrant officer mooning around the deck with a mournful overcharged air but still wearing gloves. 'Sometimes I've been seventeen days,' he says.

31 December

Apparently at ten last night excitement was caused by the sight of either an island or a ship blazing with lights on the horizon. Light in our black-out progress is like something from Jules Verne. It turns out to have been a Spanish or Portuguese liner* – the first out-of-door lights we have seen since leaving land.

The Commodore's ship overtakes us soon after break-fast, and then the first sign of land, the coast appears – not a seabird but a Sunderland flying boat taking a look round for submarines. We feel very cheerful when we see it, as though up to now we had been lost on the empty sea.

Last night a nightmare again. A friend accidentally draws a breadknife across his throat and cuts it. He lifts up the flap of flesh to see how serious it is. Taking him to hospital I see a woman in a car knock down a small boy of my son's age at the kerb and she then walked on him accidentally. The skin is wrinkled up exposing the red raw apple cheek.

---

* How these Portuguese liners were to bedevil my life – and Scobie's – at Freetown: the endless searches for commercial diamonds or for mail. No diamonds were ever found and the mail always seemed harmless enough. There was one episode of brief excitement when the Colonial Secretary had to be persuaded to ask the Navy to intercept a liner that was already safely out beyond the boom and on the edge of the three-mile limit because of a suspected spy on board: an occasion when the address-book of a suspected passenger contained the name of my friend and translator in France, Denyse Clairouin. (She was to be arrested later as a British agent and died in a German concentration camp.)

The convoy changes direction sharply and for a moment it looks as though we were going on alone. A very lonely feeling.

New Year's Eve drunk party. The cook brings in his jazz band, playing with ladles and cooking pots. Daniel the black steward dances in the passage and twists his legs round his neck. The steward falls down in the galley during a wrestling match and cuts his head open. Fish and chip supper. Broke up at 2.30 a.m.

1 January 1942

The Pole discusses with gleaming eye the advantage of having three wives. 'One wife, she rule. Three, I am king.'

2 January

Seaplane with us all day. The convoy divides. Some ships with railway engines on the decks make for the Cape. Eleven of us are left with escorts.

A very hot night brings back the subject of polygamy. Somebody asks the Pole, 'How would you manage with your three wives on a night like this?'

'Ah, you think of European passion. *Passion Orientale* not like that. There is grass, fountain. Big bed in the garden.'

Apparently about 11 p.m. a submarine was detected sixty miles off. Another rumour is that four days ago we were followed for some time.

3 January

Another large convoy of big ships hull down ahead of us – perhaps transports.

Very hot. About 10 a.m. in the mist and heat the hills behind Freetown. Before noon we had entered the boom. The great bay crowded with shipping. The strange bubble-like mountains, the yellow beaches, the absurd Anglican cathedral built of laterite bricks in the shape of a Norman church. It felt odd and poetic and encouraging coming back after so many years, a shape imposing itself on life again after chaos. It was like seeing a place you've dreamed of. Even the sweet hot smell from the land – is it the starved greenery and the red soil, the bougainvillea, the smoke from the huts in Kru town, or the fires in the bush clearing the ground for planting? – was strangely familiar. It will always be to me the smell of Africa, and Africa will always be the Africa of the Victorian atlas, the blank unexplored continent the shape of the human heart.

MORE ABOUT PENGUINS, PELICANS
AND PUFFINS

For further information about books available from Penguins please write to Dept EP, Penguin Books Ltd, Harmondsworth, Middlesex UB7 0DA.

In the U.S.A.: For a complete list of books available from Penguins in the United States write to Dept DG, Penguin Books, 299 Murray Hill Parkway, East Rutherford, New Jersey 07073.

In Canada: For a complete list of books available from Penguins in Canada write to Penguin Books Canada Limited, 2801 John Street, Markham, Ontario L3R 1B4.

In Australia: For a complete list of books available from Penguins in Australia write to the Marketing Department, Penguin Books Australia Ltd, P.O. Box 257, Ringwood, Victoria 3134.

In New Zealand: For a complete list of books available from Penguins in New Zealand write to the Marketing Department, Penguin Books (N.Z.) Ltd, Private Bag, Takapuna, Auckland 9.

In India: For a complete list of books available from Penguins in India write to Penguin Overseas Ltd, 706 Eros Apartments, 56 Nehru Place, New Delhi 110019.

GRAHAM GREENE

THE POWER AND THE GLORY

Too human for heroism, too humble for martyrdom, the little,
worldly, Mexican 'whisky priest' is impelled towards his
squalid Calvary as much by his own compassion for humanity
as by the efforts of his pursuers during an anticlerical purge.

THE QUIET AMERICAN

A terrifying portrait of innocence at large and a comment on
foreign interference in Vietnam.

THE END OF THE AFFAIR

This frank, intense account of a love-affair tells of the strange
and callous steps taken by a middle-aged writer to destroy, or
perhaps to reclaim, the mistress who had unaccountably left
him eighteen months before.

Also published

*Brighton Rock   A Burnt-Out Case
Collected Essays   The Comedians
England Made Me   A Gun for Sale
The Heart of the Matter   Twenty-One Stories
It's a Battlefield   Journey Without Maps
Loser Takes All   The Man Within
May We Borrow Your Husband?   The Ministry of Fear
Our Man in Havana   The Third Man
The Fallen Idol   Travels With My Aunt*

LUCKY JIM
Kingsley Amis

The hilarious send-up of academic life which helped to set the style of post-war fiction and placed one of today's most popular novelists firmly on course for fame.

'*Lucky Jim* deserves all the recognition it has won. It is highly intelligent and very funny' – C. P. Snow in the *Sunday Times*

LOVE FOR LYDIA
H. E. Bates

'All the happiness and the sorrow of young people in love is put in its correct perspective by the maturity and skill of a born storyteller' – Alan Melville

Lydia, a girl from a wealthy but isolated background, gradually discovers the delights of growing up – completely captivating the young men who are her companions.

The lives of the young people unfold against the carefree background of the late twenties, with summers at their hottest and winters at their coldest. It is a glimpse back at an age not long gone, but nonetheless gone forever.

CHANGING PLACES
David Lodge

The plate-glass, concrete jungle of Euphoria State University, USA, and the damp red-brick University of Rummidge have an annual exchange scheme. Normally the exchange passes without comment.

But when Philip Swallow swaps with Professor Zapp the fates play a hand, and the two academics find themselves enmeshed in a spiralling involvement on opposite sides of the Atlantic. Nobody is immune: students, colleagues, even wives are swapped as the tension increases.

'Three star rating for a laugh a line' – Auberon Waugh in the *Evening Standard* (London)

BURGER'S DAUGHTER
Nadine Gordimer

'The book has a passionate urgency and suspense, rich, intimate, even confessional . . . a beautifully manipulated work of art, moving towards a tragic and triumphant resolution' – Anthony Thwaite in the *Observer*

In this brilliantly realized work Nadine Gordimer unfolds the story of a young woman's slowly evolving identity in the turbulent political environment of present-day South Africa. The prison death of her father Lionel leaves Rosa Burger alone to explore the intricacies of what it really means to be Burger's daughter.

LOVERS OF THEIR TIME
AND OTHER STORIES
William Trevor

'I enjoyed and admired every page of it' – John Fowles

With the lightness, grace and wit that characterizes his work, William Trevor has once again produced a masterly collection of stories that will stir and haunt the imagination.

'Uniformly excellent – funny; and sad, and beautifully evocative of time and place, whether the setting is England or Ireland' – *Observer*

THE TWYBORN AFFAIR
Patrick White

Eddie Twyborn is bisexual and beautiful, the son of a Judge and a drunken mother. With this androgynous hero – Eudoxia/Eddie/Eadith Twyborn – and through his search for identity, for self-affirmation and love in its many forms, Patrick White takes us on a journey into the ambiguous landscapes, sexual, psychological and spiritual, of the human condition.

'It challenges comparison with some of the world's most bizarre masterpieces' – Isobel Murray in the *Financial Times*

SIR ARTHUR CONAN DOYLE

A STUDY IN SCARLET

'There's the scarlet thread of murder running through the colourless skein of life and our duty is to unravel it, and isolate it, and expose every inch of it.'

In this, their first adventure, Sherlock Holmes and Dr Watson uncover a thrilling story of murder, love and revenge, which began years before in Salt Lake City ...

THE SIGN OF FOUR

Following the strange disappearance of her father, Miss Morstan has received each year a mysterious present of a rare and lustrous pearl. Now, on the day of the summons to meet her anonymous benefactor, she arrives at 221B Baker Street to consult the great detective Sherlock Holmes.

With startling rapidity the mystery deepens, developing into a thrilling chase down London's streets and waterways, in pursuit of a priceless hoard of Indian treasure – and of the murderer whose ominous trademark is 'the sign of the four' ...

and

The Adventures of Sherlock Holmes
The Memoirs of Sherlock Holmes
The Return of Sherlock Holmes
The Hound of the Baskervilles